PUBLISHED *by*
PARABLES
Earthly Stories with a Heavenly Meaning

E

Strategic Methods

for a Successful Marriage

Dr. Daniel Ray Middlebrooks

PUBLISHED *by* PARABLE
Earthly Stories with a Heavenly Meaning

All Scriptural quotations are from the New International Version (NIV) unless otherwise noted. The New International Version Study Bible (Grand Rapids: Zondervan, 1985).

First Edition   January, 2017

ISBN 978-1-945698-17-0
Printed in the United States of America

Readers should be aware that Internet Web sites offered as citations and/or sources for further information may have been changed or disappeared between the time this was written and when it is read.

Illustration provided by www.unsplash.com

Strategic Methods

for a

Successful

Marriage

DR. DANIEL RAY MIDDLEBROOKS

PUBLISHED *by* PARABLES
Earthly Stories with a Heavenly Meaning

TABLE OF CONTENTS

OVERVIEW

What is the difference between a commitment to marriage and a covenant relationship in marriage? How will couples beat the 50-50 odds of marriage or divorce? The "Tested Training for the First Year" is a program that stresses the importance of couples focusing their strength and attention to the development of this crucial new relationship called marriage.

In this concept based program, three United States Army training phases, Basic Combat Training (BCT), Advanced Individual Training (AIT), and On-The-Job-Training (OJT) are used as templates for three marriage training phases for couples during the first year of matrimony. These marriage phases, Basic Marriage Training (BMT), Almighty's Marriage Training (AMT), and On-The-Job-Marriage-Training (OJMT) teach eight key elements for developing a strong relationship commitment during the first year of marriage.

In BMT, the couples learn about temperaments and four marital adjustments: emotional, mental, physical, and spiritual. This section focuses on personality differences, communication, conflict management, intimacy, and a biblical covenant marriage. This phase generally takes four months.

In the AMT phase, couples learn the importance of godly self esteem, godly discipleship, and godly responsibilities. It is here that spouses learn the power of God's love in their lives as pictured by a triangle of marriage. A couple's walk together in faith and their understanding of marital roles and expectations aid the husband and wife in a personal and inter-personal growth. As they grow closer to God they will grow closer to each other. This phase take approximately four months.

During the OJMT phase, couples learn skills for the home, children, and finances. The transition from husband and wife to dad and mom will create new stressors in the marital cycle. These lessons provide parental tools for building a strong home. Finances will be an additional stressor but couples are guided in establishing budgets and boundaries for a secure financial present that provides for the future family. This phase take four months to complete.

This cycle-style program allows couples to enter at any point of the three phases. For example, if a couple came in at the *Self Esteem* lesson during the AMT phase, they would stay until the same lesson began again a year later. This program will have increased positive impacts for couples because it causes couples to face tough questions and provides peer groups of other couples and teachers to help and encourage them.

This program is extremely useful for military families and Soldiers who are deployed. Chaplains may use these one-year lessons to assist Soldiers and family members in personal growth, while providing information for both Soldier and spouse to share every week. This will greatly enhance the reunion and re-integration of the soldier back into the family after any deployment.

This program was tested during the years of 1992-1995 in two civilian churches and from 1997-2003 in two military chapels. It was extremely utilized during deployments to Sinai, Egypt, Kosovo, and Iraq.

DEDICATION

This project would not be possible without the incredible contributions of many important people in my life. First, I would like to give praise and honor to my Lord, Jesus Christ, who is the Author and Finisher of not only my faith but of this program.

I also would like to dedicate this work to my most priceless treasures this side of heaven, my family. My wife, Arienne, who has loved, sacrificed and taught beside me these past 29 years. You are the inspiration in my life and the song of love on my lips. My two precious gifts from God, Erica and Allison. Thank you both for helping me understand my responsibility as a dad and for keeping me accountable to practice what I preach. My parents, Lloyd and Mary Ann Middlebrooks who symbolize the very description of "Eternal Newlyweds" even after 63 years of marriage. Thank you for your example of incredible commitment in marriage through all times of life.

I also want to express my thanks to the inspiring staff at Erskine Theological Seminary, especially my academic advisor DR. R.J. Gore for his patience, persistence, and professionalism. Your experience and desire for excellence enhanced my writing and has been the cheering voice that has enabled me to finish the race strong.

I deeply appreciate Jane Mayer for her constant review, editing, and time during this long process of writing. Your attention to detail is only matched by gracious desire to serve. To the staff at the Command General Staff College, Fort Belvoir, VA., thank you for your assistance in reading and providing important feedback for this program. I would also like to thank the U.S. States Army Chaplain Corp for this incredible opportunity to advance my education and expertise. I especially want to thank my former Chief of Chaplains and mentor, Chaplain (MG-Ret) Doug Carver for his counsel, his inspiration and godly example for me.

Finally, I want to thank the couples that participated in the project's research. Your love and support of my family and me through these years have been a cherished gift. Gordon and Jane Rose, my "Newlywed Mentors" from 1987 to 1992. Your words of wisdom, prayers and scriptural teaching of God's foundation of marriage are instrumental in this projects' song of success.

Pro Deo Et Patria- For God and Country!

ABBREVIATIONS

AIT	Advanced Individual Training
AMT	Almighty Marriage Training
AWOL	Absence without Leave
BCT	Basic Combat Training
BLUF	Bottom Line Up Front
BMT	Basic Marriage Training
BSRF	Building Strong and Ready Families
GMO	General Medical Orientation
MOS	Military Occupational Skill
NCOIC	Non-Commissioned Officer in Charge
OJMT	On-The-Job Marriage Training
OJT	On-The-Job Training
PT	Physical Training
SOAP	Subjective, Objective, Assessment, Procedures
SOP	Standard Operating Procedures
TRADOC	Training and Doctrine Command

INTRODUCTION

MILITARY PRACTICES

When the Army wants to take an ordinary citizen and turn him or her into a military soldier, the Army turns to Training and Doctrine Command (TRADOC). TRADOC's mission is to "Recruit, train and educate the Army's soldiers and build the future for the nation."

The centerpiece of TRADOC is the training phases each soldier goes through to make them physically, mentally, and emotionally tough for the challenges in a military culture. The training and educational phases prepare the future force by immersing the new recruits into the new culture, language, and mindset of the military. This change is not unlike the culture clash of two individuals coming together in the world of matrimony. Here two people from two unique perspectives and usually with different marriage expectations are thrust together adjusting from a single-minded life to a marriage mindset. There is an amazing similarity between the training, education, and development of a military soldiers and the integration of two "becoming one" in marriage. If that is true, how will military practices apply to the principles of marriage? Allow me to describe the setting for this project.

The plane landed and I walked through the terminal to the designated meeting place for all soldiers attending Basic Training at Fort Jackson, S.C. There were approximately twenty in all as we boarded the bus and went to our new home. The training I was about to receive would be a year-long and it would be broken down into three primary phases.[1]

The first phase was Basic Combat Training (BCT). In the first few days, the recruits are housed in an area labeled the Reception Station. Here you receive various supplies, clothes, and some instruction. It is a semi-relaxed environment. You learn a little about marching and the rank structures and you can eat anything you want. It is a type of "honeymoon" experience. While at the reception station at Fort Jackson, I heard others express, "Hey, this Basic Training is not bad at all!" I looked at them and said, "Buddy, this isn't Basic

Training. This is the calm before the storm!" I hate being right! After four days, the honeymoon stage turned into the horror stage. The people that were nice to us suddenly turned mean. It was like being in the twilight zone. We moved from the serene atmosphere of the Reception Station to the stress-filled world of the Training area. I asked myself, "What in the world did I get myself into?"

In the training area of BCT, the Drill Instructors had two training concepts: *self-examination and team integration.* The first concept, self-examination, was to help someone discover his or her true self. This was achieved by breaking a person down physically, emotionally, and mentally. During this time of internal inspection, one realized what type of person he or she was. This process helped answer the questions, *"How will I react to different challenging circumstances?"* and *"What am I made of?"* Some new soldiers do not make it through this initial stage of training. In his book, *Basic Training For a Few Good Men,* Tim Kimmel expressed, "You can't count the number of enlistees who have wished they could go absent without leave (AWOL) from boot camp long enough to slap their recruiters silly. All of the pride, nobility, and romance that the recruiter talked about are hard to imagine when you're hip deep in some swamp, wearing fifty pounds on your back, and only halfway through a fifteen-mile hike."[2] The stress and strain of this new environment is too great for some soldiers to handle and they are discharged from military service.

The second concept, team integration, was to develop a one-team mentality. It was through the principle of external connections that teams learned to *"shoot, move and communicate"* as one mind and body. It was in this phase of training that I developed the ability to work with others in any given situation. It also reinforced that the power of two or more is better than the strength of one. Through a series of training exercises, skill-honing programs, and team-building practices, the one-team mentality was formed and became an unstoppable force.

The second phase was Advanced Individual Training (AIT). During this phase one learned the required skills for a future job. The training, however, was not the sole responsibility of the drill sergeant but now rested on the student. Success and failure rested on what one thought about self-discipline, maturity, and initiative. The internal attitudes and motivation would either take one to the top of this rugged mountain of schooling or simply cause one to stay in the flatlands of defeated shadows. The AIT phase of training was divided into three training concepts: *Preliminary Training, Textbook Training,* and *Technical Ttraining.* First was the preliminary training. It was at this stage that you received an overall understanding of the job in which you were about to be trained. If you could not pass this portion of the training, you would not go on to the next. Before I entered into my 91J Physical Therapy Military Occupational Specialty (MOS) training, I had to complete the General Medical Orientation

(GMO) schooling. If I could not grasp the simple concepts of the heart and body system, there would be little chance for me to go deeper into the areas of physical therapy. Simply, if I did not like the sight of blood, there was no need to pursue further training in the medical field!

Second was the textbook training. This area concentrated on the information that was vital for successful integration into one's job. While going through the 91J schooling, the information of the body systems and the various therapy treatment plans were explained and diagrammed throughout the pages of the manuals. The last concept was the technical training. During this time, one would learn the needed resources for successful execution of his or her job. Many tests and practical examinations helped a soldier demonstrate an understanding of the skills required for graduation. As in BCT, some soldiers did not make it. Many suffered from a lack of personal determination to push through the challenges and trials of this phase. Only those committed to push themselves onward and upward gained success.

The third phase is on-the-job-training (OJT). It is during the OJT phase that book knowledge met real-life application. There are three main concepts in this final phase of military training: *Practicing the Principles, Perfecting the Techniques,* and *Preparing for the Future.* First, practicing the principles of the job means everything that was taught and tested is now used and applied. This is the truest test of one's knowledge. A person can be a great test-taker but a terrible skill-demonstrator. Second is the perfecting of the techniques. Everyone has his or her own style in how they perform their job. The military manuals teach a model to follow but it is the individual abilities and talents that seal the skills in our life. This is where two "R"s are important: "*Repetition and Review.*" To do the skill over and over and over converts it from a principle to a practice.

The third concept is preparing for the future. As one moves to the end of the training, policies and procedures are now a part of everyday life. Whereas one reads the standard operating procedures (SOP) when first arriving at a hospital, one can now recall them by heart and implement the procedures effectively. Life is a constant state of learning and one should never settle for the current level of knowledge. One needs to strive constantly to learn and to do more in life because life is a continuous teacher. Still, some struggle to make it through this time. Although the number is not as great as in the first two phases, there will be those who will call it quits. They become disenchanted with the job, lose their motivation, or dream about their life before the military. With this setting in mind, I will explain how these military practices correspond to marriage principles.

Marriage Principles

Basic Marriage Training

When two people join their lives in marriage under God, they step into a new world. It is when they have been "sworn in" and say the words, "I do," that they enter into the Basic Marriage Training (BMT) phase of marriage. Even though newlyweds may date for a number of years, one never truly knows someone until married. The first days or weeks will feel like the honeymoon time at the Reception Station. It is great being married. The status, the recognition, and the feeling of becoming a "man or woman," tint the windows of our souls . . . for a time. Then, the "Horror Stage" appears. The man that you thought you knew as "Prince Charming" while dating has suddenly become "Shrek" overnight. The "Cinderella" that you searched the countryside for seems to have turned into one of the selfish and ugly stepsisters. Life has changed suddenly and your head and heart are spinning with the questions, "What did I do?"

Like the military basic combat training, a person in BMT will learn more about himself in this time of emotional, mental, and physical testing. As stated earlier, the skills to survive the military BCT included understanding one's self (self examination) and then understanding others (team integration). For the marriage to survive past the beginning months, these same skills are needed. "In God's plan, our differences were never intended to divide us. In fact, God is the author of diversity . . . . When He instituted marriage as a union of two unique individuals, He knew that He was creating unity out of diversity."[3] As a man examines himself internally, he also learns to adjust and work with another externally. This is *team-integration* turning into marriage integration. Life is easier when one is alone; however, when married one has another person in life to consider. This can be a difficult transition. Through constant emotional, mental, physical, and spiritual adjustments, one will learn how to "*share, mature, and communicate.*" The two hearts and minds become one. This is not the loss of the individual personalities but the connecting and complementing of each other as a new team, a new family. "Many marriages would be better if the husband and the wife clearly understood that they are on the same side."[4] Such an understanding and commitment to these differences will radically improve the marriage relationship and pave a way for the next phase of marriage.

ALMIGHTY'S MARRIAGE TRAINING

The Almighty's Marriage Training (AMT) stage is the preparation platform for a husband and wife to move from the focus of two minds and hearts to a life and faith of one. God, through His Son Jesus Christ, invites all to follow Him both as individuals and as a couple. Through His scriptures, He presents the guidelines and training lessons for one of the greatest and most challenging positions one will ever hold in life, a husband or wife. The internal desire and disciplines needed for a couple to walk in faith may be difficult but render incredible dividends. Like the military AIT stage, the three concepts of preliminary training, textbook training, and technical training apply here. In the preliminary training, this concept concentrates on one's self-image and acceptance from God. The principles of worth, high value, and blessings are present in this stage.

What do we mean by "Worth and High Value"? To value something means to attach great importance, or worth, to it. This is the very heart of a concept called "the blessing" in marriage. John Trent explains, "The root word of value is used of a man who has his camel bend its knees. Bowing before someone is a picture of honor and of valuing the person. Notice the important principle here. Anytime we bless someone, we are attaching high value to him or her."[5] If you cannot learn to accept the love, grace, and worth God has provided for you, there is no need to move onto the next level of training. This first concept is the cornerstone of success for the AMT phase. When spouses feel valued by God, this opens the door to a deeper faith in and discipleship for God.

The second training concept deepens one's walk of faith and the call to discipleship. Whereas the military AIT uses an Army textbook to understand the program, AMT uses the Bible to understand one's purpose. Consider the image of a triangle with the husband and the wife at the two bottom corners, one left and one right. Place God at the top of the triangle. With this mental picture, movement of each spouse toward God will produce a wonderful result. As each spouse draws closer to God, they will draw closer to each other. It is the journey toward God that impacts all the present and future areas of training.

The third concept, technical training, is the understanding and acceptance of the various responsibilities of a husband and wife. Couples may enter into marriage with a wide range of expectations which, if left unstated, can and will cause conflict. The technical training of godly responsibilities fine tunes the clarity of marriage roles for each spouse in the relationship. This not only gathers relationship resources for success but instructs spouses in loving service to God, spouse, and family. The roles of the man and woman help establish a godly legacy for the next generations to come. The flow of these three marriage AMT concepts can be summed up in these three words: *Worth, Worship,* and *Walk.*

On-The-Job Marriage Training

The last stage of training is the One-the-Job Marriage Training (OJMT). This arena of training deals with home, children, and finances. The three steps of practicing, perfecting, and preparing found the military OJT are valid for this OJMT phase. First, one will practice the marriage principles. During this training concept, one learns how to move from *lip service* to *life service*. It is very important that both spouses are working toward the same goal of home policies and application. As one author noted, "The only rules in a marriage are those to which you both choose to agree."[6]

Second, through consistency and continuity, one is able to perfect marriage techniques. Especially when it comes to children, the power of the unified front of both mom and dad cannot be underestimated. This training concept quite literally is on-the-job training. It is during this hands-on application that one learns the most. One may have read multiple parenting manuals but when the learned principles are put into action, one will discover the principles are easier preached than practiced. Third, and lastly, one prepares for the future of marriage by focusing on finances. One cannot expect to live a champagne lifestyle on a root beer budget. To learn the discipline to say "No" to the quick fix and "Yes" to the best solution allows a couple to experience financial freedom in marriage instead of the bondage of bills. Again, as explained earlier, some will drop out of this phase saying that it was not what they expected, anticipated, or wanted. The crucial aspects of this stage are when couples come face to face with their family of origin issues, positive or negative parenting styles, and financial decisions.

BOTTOM LINE UP FRONT

A favorite military term is BLUF meaning "bottom line up front." When discussing courses of action for an event or tactical maneuver, the BLUF becomes important when time is of the essence to make a decision. The following sections will give you the BLUF of the chapters developed and the resources used for this project. The diagram on page 12 provides a visual picture relating to the chapter breakdown

A favorite military term is BLUF meaning "bottom line up front." When discussing courses of action for an event or tactical maneuver, the BLUF becomes important when time is of the essence to make a decision. The following sections will give you the BLUF of the chapters developed and the resources used for this project. The diagram on page 20 provides a visual picture relating to the chapter breakdown.

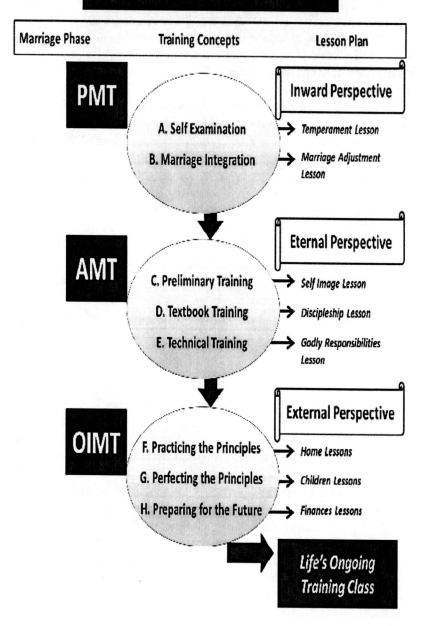

CHAPTER BREAKDOWN

Chapter one will focus on the biblical foundations for the newlywed project, "Two Minds, One Master." The chapter will consider three biblical perspectives; *Inward, Upward,* and *Outward,* as they relate to the three training phases of BMT, AMT, and OJMT in the project. The inward perspective will examine the scriptural nature of temperaments and marriage adjustments found in the BMT phase. It will consider three questions regarding the commitment for marriage, the completeness in marriage, and the covenant of marriage. Second, the upward perspective will explore the faith relationships of God and the couple through the lessons of self-image, discipleship, and godly responsibilities as found in the AMT phase. This section will ask and answer the questions, *What does God think of me? How do I worship God? How will my spouse and I walk with and serve God together?* The external perspective, found in the OJMT phase, will concentrate on the biblical principles of home, children, and finances. This section will cover the scriptural principles for godly boundaries in marriage for spouses, children, and extended family. I will also explore the power and impact of a godly legacy in marriage.

Chapter two will discuss the BCT phase of self-examination and marriage integration. I will explain the impact of a couples' understanding of temperament styles along with strengths and weaknesses. I will also help couples understand the important adjustments emotionally, mentally, physically, and spiritually needed in marriage. These adjustments will explore many factors such as communication techniques, conflict management, and a healthy sex life. For example, in the military BCT, the soldier is trained on the use of his weapon for defense and attack. In the marriage BMT, we often trade the metal weapon of war for a mental weapon of words. These tend to do far more immediate and long lasting damage. Words, like hammers, can either be used constructively or destructively. How one communicates is determined by one's understanding, experience, and practice of communication. One's model of conflict management will also form a personal approach to communication. It is therefore important to examine the roots and reactions of conflict in life as these will impact the words used in marriage. As Gary Smalley expressed in his book, *Secrets to Lasting Love*, "Most people view conflict as negative. Many can't stand disagreement in any form. And so, to avoid conflict, they avoid expressing their opinions and hope that their mate will do the same." [7] This quiet rigidity will also have an effect on the sexual relationship of the marriage. "If we are going to reclaim sexuality, the first hurdle we must overcome is the difficulty of talking clearly and openly about it." [8] This phase of training is foundational for *"two heads"* becoming *"one heart."*

Chapter three, the AMT phase, will focus on the preliminary training (*eternal worth*), Bible textbook training (*worship*), and technical training (*spiritual walk of marriage*). First, the foundation of a strong love in marriage is in the internal values and

worth one brings to marriage. During this focus of eternal worth, the reader will discover the triad of marriage. This triad is best illustrated in a triangle of marriage. This triangle will explain the flow of self-esteem and worth from God to self and from the self to the spouse. For example, if a wife does not see herself as having worth from God, she may be reluctant to receive the love she needs from her husband. She may also be unable to truly express love to her husband. It is not that she does not desire to love but her low self-worth acts like a cap that closes off love coming in or going out. "Honor is a way of accurately seeing the immense value of someone made in the image of God. God created each one of us as a one-of-a-kind person . . . . When we see others as God sees them and when we recognize and affirm their value, we help create a safe environment that encourages relationships to grow." [9] Second, this chapter will teach the importance of spiritual worship and discipleship as a couple. Although it is important to have a private devotional discipline, couple devotions and Bible studies will generate a strong spiritual growth toward and with each spouse. Once a husband and wife realize the impact of faith in marriage, they will be able to understand and live out the godly responsibilities of marriage.

Chapter four concludes the project with the OJMT phase of external attitudes and applications. First, in relationship to practicing the marriage principles, I explain family development and how different principles can create a healthy or hurting home. Linda and Charlie Bloom in their book, *101 things I Wish I Knew When I Got Married*, said, "Growing up in a happy marriage doesn't ensure a good marriage and growing up in an unhappy family doesn't preclude having one." [10] It is not how you started out in life but how you want to end up in life that will matter. There may be cycles, family roles, and traditions that you may choose to keep and there may be some that you desire to protect your new family from. Secondly, to perfect the techniques in marriage, I will discuss the establishment of boundaries. These boundaries should be in place regarding the family home, the spouse, children, and the extended family. Why is it important to talk about the in-laws? Consider this thought from Leonard Felder: "Each of us has a unique family, and yet there are certain personality types and typical conflicts that show up in millions of families."[11] Last, I describe how spouses financially prepare for the future of their home and family through the avenue of teachings for financial responsibility.

Chapter five presents the feedback of various couples that have attended this year-long training. Each couple was presented a survey and two couples were personally interviewed. The desire from this research survey was to discover the effect of the training made during the beginning of their marriage to their present stage of marriage. A range of questions covered a variety of areas including class lessons, knowledge of marriage principles before and after the training, and the possible marriage sustaining impacts in their relationship for over ten years period of time.

Chapter six provides a short conclusion for the research, some closing personal reflections and factors from the newlywed classes.

Cited Marriage Resources

The "Tested Training for the First Year" is a primary concept that stresses the importance of couples focusing their strength and attention to the development of this crucial new relationship. The following is a summary of some of the relevant authors and resources covered in this research.

Throughout the entire newlywed curriculum, one author is prominent. Gary Smalley has developed more than forty books and has worked with couples for the last more than thirty years. Although the list is long, the primary resources for this research are *The Language of Love, Making Love Last Forever, The Hidden Value of a Man, The Blessing,* and *The Two Sides of Love.* The first book teaches the impact of word pictures. The ability to paint a picture when communicating issues with your spouse is powerful. During the formation of my marriage, this techniques of sharing my hurts, needs, and love in a word picture for my wife took the normal conversation of marriage to another level. Smalley states, "If we're serious about having meaningful, fulfilling, productive relationships, we can't afford to let inadequate communication skills carry our conversations."[12]

In the second book, Smalley describes two primary loves in our marriage. The first is the need to fall in love with life. The second is staying in love with your spouse. He also explores the issues of anger, personalities, and the marriage manual of each spouse and how these issues impact the understanding of temperament and marriage adjustments. The third resource focuses the energy toward the man and the responsibilities of being both tender and tough. The pictures of two swords line the pages and describe the tension of a positional power and a personal power. In the sections on Self-Esteem, Responsibilities and Home, he says the husband and father can make or break a marriage by the usage of only the sword of positional power. "If we have grown up with our father's acceptance at arms' length, we can easily shove our families away as well."[13] Once a husband and father understands the importance of his role, he will be able to give a blessing to his family as noted in Smalley's *The Blessing*. The last of the books is an insightful examination of the personality traits that exists within a family. Smalley and John Trent take an inventive approach, using the characteristics of various animals to describe the four temperament traits of Sanguine (Otter), Choleric (Lion), Melancholy (Golden Retriever), and Phlegmatic (Beaver). The understanding of temperament strengths and weaknesses helps couples to understand how each experiences life. A helpful insight is that weaknesses are usually strengths "pushed to an extreme."[14]

Another significant figure in the field of family and marriage is James Dobson. His family resources, *Dare to Discipline* and *Parenting Isn't for Cowards*, are foundational for the growth of strong and healthy homes. The various workbooks and videos that sprinkle throughout the chapters are too numerous to explain. One unique resource for couples in the area of discipleship is his devotional book, *Night Light*. The power behind this book is that couples read it together. The devotions take less than ten minutes and ask specific questions regarding the topic read. This not only opens up the avenues of communication between spouses but also assists the foundation of prayer and faith. This resource can also be used while a couple is away from each other.

In his book, *The Five Love Languages*, Gary Chapman masterfully describes the need of communicating the right way to our spouses. This book was especially helpful in the Adjustment section of study. In teaching communication, the ability to discover your love language is only the first step. The premise of expressing love as one enjoys being loved is common sense but often over-looked. For couples to know their love language opens the door to endless possibilities of nurturing and growing a marriage. In various marriage retreats in the military where time is short, these principles are easily taught and spouses receive immediate feedback to its application. As Chapman and Ross Campbell explain in their book, *The Five Love Languages of Children*, these principles also apply easily with the youngest members of the family. Although most children would not be able to take the assessment tool, the parent can watch how the child expresses love to the parent. Chapman says, "By speaking your child's love language, you can fill his emotional tank with love. When your child feels loved, he is much easier to discipline and train . . . ."[15]

Henry Cloud and John Townsend bring a host of practical information and important impacts in their various boundaries series. The most powerful ones in the newlywed curriculum are *Boundaries in Marriage* and *Boundaries with Kids*. These show the imperative of establishing protective parameters which are essential to an environment of healthy growth in both marriage and child rearing. Marriage and family boundaries do not ensure the absence of conflict but allows couples to disagree without becoming disagreeable. Cloud explains, "The marriage relationship needs other ingredients to grow and thrive. Those ingredients are freedom and responsibility. When two people are free to disagree, they are free to love."[16]

So, if you are ready to step forward into this intensive training program, please raise your right hand and repeat after me, "I DO!"

CHAPTER ONE

THE BIBLICAL FOUNDATION OF MARRIAGE

THE "POWER" OF THE FIRST YEAR

If a man has recently married, he must not be sent to war or have any other duty laid on him. For one year he is to be free to stay at home and bring happiness to the wife he has married (Deuteronomy 24:5).[17]

What would this nation's marriages be like if couples were allowed to take the very first year and have only one focus: to establish a strong marriage. It would probably have a devastating effect on the divorce courts and lawyers of the land. Yet that was the very practice that God established for the children of Israel during the time of Moses. It was a primary marital task for Jewish men to have children so their legacy and name would continue. This principle seems, however, much deeper than this simple explanation. Otherwise, the passage might have read, "free to stay home so that there will be a child." Much has changed from the perspective of marriage in the Old Testament to today's matrimony. The average time that a couple will truly spend concentrating on the marriage will be approximately one month, and that includes the honeymoon. This is a sad change from the strong biblical foundation of the covenant marriage of Adam and Eve's "leaving and cleaving" to the current contractual approach of pre-marriage counseling and marriage relationships. Eric Ludy, co-author of *The First 90 Days of Marriage*, described marriage in the beginning months to be that of "moist and malleable clay." Once this clay hardens, it is hard to change.[18] This first foundation, the covenant marriage, establishes a couple's ability to weather any stress or storm in life, especially during the first year of marriage.

MARRIAGE FOUNDATIONS OR FAILURES

According to *Divorce Magazine*, "Statistics tell us that about half of all marriages now end in divorce."[19] A challenger to this statement is Jim Killam of *Christianity Today*. He writes, "Recent research suggests that one marriage in four is closer to the true divorce rate. The 50-percent myth originated a couple of decades ago when someone looked at marriage and divorce numbers reported by the National Center for Health Statistics. The number of divorces in one year was precisely half the number of marriages. *Voila!* Half of all marriages end in divorce."[20] Killam continues to explain that there are flaws in various statistics.

A lot of people are alive who neither were born nor died this year. You very likely are one of them. Similarly, the divorce statisticians forgot to figure in the marriages already in existence, of which there are millions. "The media, frankly, tend to use a lot of information without ever challenging what they use," says researcher George Barna, author of *The Future of the American Family*. So the media can shoulder much of the blame for propagating an inaccurate statistic.[21] While it is good to hear the positive number of marriages over divorces, it is alarming to discover that Christians are experiencing the same rate of divorce as non-Christians. This pattern, according to George Barna, has been in place for quite some time.[22] Even more disturbing, perhaps, is that when those individuals experience a divorce, many of them feel their community of faith provides rejection rather than support and healing. The research also raises questions regarding the effectiveness of churches' ministries to families. The ultimate responsibility for a marriage belongs to the husband and wife, but the high incidence of divorce within the Christian community challenges the idea that churches provide truly practical and life-changing support for marriages. Christians Have Same Incidence of Divorce

Although many Christian churches attempt to dissuade congregants from getting a divorce, the research confirmed a finding identified by Barna a decade ago. "Christians have the same likelihood of divorce, as do non-Christians. Among married born-again Christians, 35% have experienced a divorce. That figure is identical to the outcome among married adults who are not born-again: 35%." [23] Barna also noted that one reason why the divorce statistic among non-religious adults is not higher is that a larger proportion of that group cohabits, effectively sidestepping marriage and divorce altogether. This may impact overall numbers. The survey continued by stating among born again adults, 80% have been married, compared to just 69% among the non-born again segment. If the non-born again population were to marry at the same rate as the born-again group, "it is likely that their divorce statistic would be roughly 38%, marginally higher than that among the born again group but still surprisingly similar in magnitude." [24]

Barna also noted that he analyzed the data according to the ages at which survey respondents were divorced and the age at which those who were Christian accepted Jesus Christ as their savior. "The data suggests that relatively few divorced Christians experienced their divorce before accepting Christ as their savior," he explained. "If we eliminate those who became Christians after their divorce, the divorce figure among born-again adults drops to 34% — statistically identical to the figure among non-Christians." [25] The researcher also indicated that a surprising number of Christians experienced divorces both before and after their conversion. Multiple divorces are also unexpectedly common among born-again Christians. Barna's figures show that nearly one-quarter of the married born-again (23%) get divorced two or more times.

Variation in Divorce Rates among Christian Faith Groups

"Even among born-again Christians, most don't exhibit attitudes or behaviors any different than non-Christians." [26] The survey showed that divorce varied somewhat by a person's denominational affiliation. Roman Catholics were substantially less likely than Protestants to get divorced (25% versus 39%, respectively). Among the largest Protestant groups, those most likely to get divorced were Pentecostals (44%) while Presbyterians had the fewest divorces (28%).

Denomination (In Order of Decreasing Divorce Rate)	% Who Have Been Divorced
Non-denominational (small conservative groups; independents)	34%
Baptists	29%
Mainline Protestants	25%
Mormons	24%
Catholics	21%
Lutherans	21%

Barna's results verified findings of earlier polls: that conservative Protestant Christians, on average, have the highest divorce rate, while mainline Christians have a much lower rate. Donald Hughes, author of *The Divorce Reality*, states the data challenges "the idea that churches provide truly practical and life-changing support for marriage." Barna also said, "In the churches, people have a superstitious view that Christianity will keep them from divorce, but they are subject to the same problems as everyone else, and they include a lack of relationship skills . . . . Just being born again is not a rabbit's foot."[27]

Barna's research is a recent attempt at finding the true divorce rate in America. The survey's margin of error is plus or minus 1 to 2 percent. Those numbers, once publicized, met with only mild surprise. Barna explains "That's the milieu they live in. Either they've been through a divorce or they know someone who has. It's no longer the shocking reality that it was 30 or 40 years ago." Again, these statistics should be explained. Barna's group asked belief-oriented questions to categorize people. Jim Mattox says regular church attendance might be a better indicator of religion's effect on marital stability, since about 80 percent of Americans consider themselves Christians and about 40 percent says they're born-again.[28] Regarding church attendance, another Barna study indicated that "Four out of every ten adults (40%) attend a church service on a typical Sunday. That figure is a significant decline from the early Nineties, when close to half of all adults were found in churches on Sunday, but the figure is relatively unchanged since 1994."[29] This survey does pose a question as to the correlation between the decrease in church attendance and the increase of divorces among Christian. Clearly, being a Christian and 'in love' is not enough for a successful marriage. All of the above statistics simple prove an age old lesson that marital happiness is not automatic. Fortunately for us, God has not left us without His help. In His word, He explains how we are to approach marriage through the love and life of His son, Jesus, and it starts with one word-covenant.

THE PURPOSE AND POWER
OF A GODLY COVENANT MARRIAGE

The marriage covenant provides us with a clue to understanding the heart of God. It helps us understand what God has done, is doing, and will do for us. It tells us that God's covenant love is a love that will not let us go. "By helping us understand the purpose and permanence of God's relationship with us, the metaphor of the marriage covenant helps us also to understand the purpose and permanence of our marital relationships. The fact that human marriages have a divine pattern provides us with a holy help in understanding how to live out our marriage covenant."[30] Covenant marriage is not a new concept. Throughout the scriptures, God's people made covenants with one another. Malachi 2:13-14 speaks directly about the marriage as a covenant relationship and the impact of disregarding this commitment.

> Another thing you do; You flood the Lord's altar with tears. You weep and wail because He no longer pays attention to your offerings or accepts them with pleasure from your hands. You ask "Why?" It is because the Lord is acting as the witness between you and the wife of your youth, because you have broken faith with her, though she is your partner, the wife of your marriage covenant.

The Lord, through the Prophet Malachi, reminded the children of Israel of the symbolic relationship between a man and a woman in marriage and the spiritual relationship between Him and the children of Israel. The witness of the covenant was the binding testimony of accountability and authority of the commitment. So, then, what is a covenant? A covenant is a "relationship bound by steadfast love, faithfulness and devotion. The heart of a covenant is not rights and responsibilities, but steadfast love which never ceases."[31] Lamentations 3:22 states, "Because of the Lord's great love we are not consumed, for His compassion never fails." In a time when the world screams about the importance and personal expectations of rights, the covenant rights and responsibilities in marriage grow out of a deep relationship characterized by steadfast love, faithfulness, and devotion. A covenant means "two people will act in love toward each other unconditionally."[32] It is not giving and receiving love as long as the other spouse measures up to expectations and desires. It is love that is freely expressed and given regardless if earned or deserved. Why the term covenant marriage? Covenant marriage "clearly denotes the uniqueness of a Christian marriage. Covenant is a biblical term. God is a covenant-making God."[33]

During times, and even as practiced today in some nomadic tribes, when a man and woman were pledged to be married, the fathers would slaughter a goat or other animal, cut the carcass in half, and then at sundown walk barefoot through the blood path. The slaughtered animals symbolized what would happen to either party if they violated the terms of the agreement. This was the ceremony God chose to use when he entered into a covenant with Abraham in Genesis 15. God asked Abram to take a heifer, a goat and a ram, plus a dove and a young pigeon, and slaughter them. There was an unusual twist in this ceremony. While Abraham and his descendants were committed to this covenant with God, only God walked the blood path, thereby signifying that if Israel violated the agreement, God would pay the price with His own blood. Today most people do not understand what the word 'covenant' means. Today's culture is built on contracts in which lawyers can find a loophole if a spouse really wants out of the marriage. So contracts get longer and longer as the parties try to close all possible loopholes, but litigation increases because people change their minds and want release from their agreements.

One contract that is increasing in usage is the prenuptial agreement. "Contracts are usually made with the idea that the arrangement will be mutually beneficial for both parties involved . . . . This contract mentality predisposes the couple to divorce when the relationship comes on hard times."[34] A covenant is not at all like a prenuptial agreement. For one thing, there is no escape clause. In ancient times, a covenant was a legal agreement, but with two major differences from contracts today. A covenant was made before God. The penalty for breaking it was death. People might negotiate out of contracts, but not out of a covenant. The covenant between God and Abraham was more binding than a wedding certificate is today.[35] God impressed on Abraham the importance of the covenant: ". . . As for you, you must keep my covenant, you and your descendants after you for the generations to come" (Genesis 17:9). God, in walking the blood pathway alone, exclaimed that He would ultimately pay the price for the infidelity of Abraham's descendants. What is the cost of marriage today?

When a couple marries today, a lot of effort goes into the wedding. According to *Bride's* magazine, when the average couple adds up the costs of a wedding dress, tuxedos, dresses for the bridesmaids, rings, invitations, flowers, music, photographer, wedding cake and reception, they spend more than $19,000.[36]

Although many fathers may look at the sum and start saving when their baby girl is born, the true cost of marriage is not in the ceremony but in the broken and shattered lives of a non-committal society that looks at marriage as a contract to be endured rather than a covenant to be lived.

Covenant relationships are based on the decision to act in accordance with love, not feelings. These eternal decisions are not the outgrowth of 'falling in love' but are, instead, a faithfulness in action. "A healthy functional couple commit to each other through the power of will. They decide and choose to stand by each other. . . . It's not some superficial feeling — it's a decision."[37] In the example of Ruth, did she feel like leaving her homeland and family after the death of her husband? She decided to hold onto her mother-in-law, Naomi, and go to a new home with a new people. There God blessed her with a kinsman-redeemer named Boaz and we see a picture of love's triumph over testing. (Ruth 1-4). To take the picture of covenant love into the New Testament, consider

Jesus in the garden of Gethsemane. As Jesus prayed, was he excited about the prospect of being crucified on the cross? (Matthew 26:36-46) Covenant love and care for each other in marriage mirrors God's love and care for the world. This type of marriage is an opportunity to witness the grace and love of the Lord as each spouse demonstrates the transforming power of God's love in the human relationships. As couples live in a covenant relationship with each other, they are, in truth, living in covenant with God. This will impact the world at large as John writes, "By this all men will know that you are my disciples, if you have love for one another" (John 13:34-35, NASB).

GOD'S DESIGN AND DESIRE FOR COUPLES

Most couples have little direct education in the art and skill of nurturing a marriage. Perhaps the most significant training one can have for marriage comes from personally observing the parents. This can either help a couple to walk toward a strong and healthy relationship or it can lead them astray to be shipwrecked later in emotional and mental despair. One's expectations of marriage, as well as ways of handling intimacy and conflict, often reflect the relationship of our parents. This is particularly true during times of stress when it is hard to think clearly about what to say or do. The following eight principles are foundational for newlyweds as they begin marriage and important for all other couples as yearly refreshers. The power of the first year, as stated earlier in the first section, concentrates the couple's attention in eight principles of marriage. These are temperaments, adjustments, self-image, discipleship, responsibilities, home, children, and finances. When couples begin to understand themselves and truly open up their minds and hearts to the understanding and practice of these timeless principles, the building of a strong marriage is inevitable.

TEMPERAMENTS

Humanly speaking, nothing has a more profound impact on human behavior than one's inherited temperament. "The combination of the parent's genes and chromosones at conception, which determine one's basic temperament nine months before a first breath is taken, is largely responsible for your actions, reactions, emotional responses, and, to a degree or another, alomost everything you do."[38] Everyone wants to know why the act the way they do! The apostle Paul expressed, "... for to will is present with me, but how to perform what is good I do not find. For the good that I will to do, I do not do; but the evil I will not to do, that I practice. Now if I do what I will not to do, it is no longer I who do it,

33

but sin that dwells in me" (Rom. 7:18-20 NKJV). Note that Paul differentiated between himself and that uncontrollable force within by saying, "It is no longer I who do it, but sin that dwells in me." The "I" is Paul's person, the soul, will, and the human mind. The "sin" that resided in him resulted from the natural weaknesses that he, like all human beings, received from his parents.

"Temperament is a configuration of inclinations. . . . Put another way, our brain is a sort of computer which has temperament for its software."[39] This software puts an "identifiable fingerprint"[40] on each person. Since temperament is inherited genetically from our parents, one should keep in mind some of the natural factors that influence it. A person's gender may affect his or her temperament, particularly in the realm of the emotions. Men and women may have the same temperament, but the extent of emotional expression may vary. One must be cautious not to stereotype aspects of a person's temperament due to gender. Marvin Minsky, author of *The Emotion Machine*, states emotion is "one of the suitcase-like words that we use to conceal the complexity of very large ranges of different things whose relationships we don't yet comprehend."[41] Temperament traits, whether controlled or uncontrolled, last throughout life. Florence Littauer, in her book, *Personality Plus*, suggests that our temperament is like a rock. "Some of us are granite, some marble, some alabaster, some sandstone. Our type of rock doesn't change, but our shapes can be altered."[42] Marriage is a chiseler of this rock. People learn that if they are to live at peace with their spouses and neighbors, it is best to emphasize their natural strengths and subdue their weaknesses. One of the most transforming aspects for a newlywed couple is for each not only to identify his or her temperament but to seek to understand the temperament of his or her spouse. Throughout the marriage, temperaments may be expressed in various ways during times of stress, grief, loss, and joy. According to Littauer, these reactions will be influenced by the various levels of strengths and/or weaknesses within each temperament.[43]

For each spouse, identifying both strengths and weaknesses should cause one to concentrate on the weak areas in his or her life rather than focus on the weakness in the life of spouses. God has a particular strength for every weakness as found in Galatians 5:22 regarding the fruit of the spirit. In marriage, a couple's weaknesses tend to come out more than at any other time. "Often, a weakness can be a strength pushed to an extreme."[44] In each person, there are traits that are positive and traits that are negative. "Quite often the same characteristic (trait) can be both a plus and a minus, according to the degree, and many positives carried to extremes become negatives."[45] An example could be the powerful Choleric. The Choleric's gift for quick, incisive leadership is needed in every phase of life, but, carried to extremes, can cause them to become bossy, controlling, and manipulative. If the Melancholy's ability for deep, analytical thinking is pushed to an extreme, he or she can become brooding and depressed. Husbands and wives must learn to let God build their character through their mate. They must also learn how to overcome their weaknesses through the power of the Holy Spirit. Myles Munroe says, "As spiritual beings created in the image of God, men and women are indeed equal.... As human beings with male and female bodies, however, their needs are distinctly different."[46] If a couple allows the Holy Spirit to be the primary chiseler of the temperament rock, the results can produce a Michelangelo masterpiece. When spouses combine the study of both scripture and temperament, the power of God's changing grace can be experienced. Some scriptures that support this perspective are Ephesians 4:30-32, Philippians 4:4-8, Psalm 27, Psalm 37, and I Thessalonians 5:16-18. Through the mind, heart, soul, spirit and life, a couple can draw closer to see the different temperaments as a gift from God rather than a curse.

In summary, a couple can see that they have both strengths and weaknesses. They can also see that a mature Christian is one who knows both his or her strengths and weaknesses and has a planned program for overcoming the weaknesses. It is important, however, to realize that in one's own power, a spouse is unable to overcome these weaknesses. Some may argue that knowing one's weaknesses is sufficient in life but this is not true. A husband and wife must have a plan for overcoming their weaknesses and must yield to the Holy Spirit to provide the power necessary for overcoming them. Once couples begin to understand how God has wired each of them with a particular temperament, the next step is to learn how to adjust to each other.

ADJUSTMENTS

"Research shows that nearly four in ten divorced persons report infidelity or incompatibility of character was the reason for their marriage breakdown. An equal amount of men and women identify these reasons as the cause of marital dissolution."[47]

Adjustment in marriage is not as much aptitude (knowing what to do) as it is attitude (the willingness to do it). In the 2000s, the number one reason for divorce in society is the inability to get along with the other spouse. In the military, it is called a "failure to adapt." In the civilian world of marriage, it is considered a failure to "adjust." There is a simple scriptural reference that sheds light on this growing problem within the world today. Jesus said that "Every kingdom divided against itself is brought to desolation, and every city or house divided against itself will not stand." (Matthew 12:25, NKJV) As couples enter into marriage, they approach marriage in one or a combination of these four ways: Intimidation, manipulation, capitulation, or adaptation. Spouses must be willing to adapt (adjust) in four crucial areas of life if they hope to find the rich fullness in marriage. As seen in *figure 1.1*, these areas are emotional, mental, physical, and spiritual.

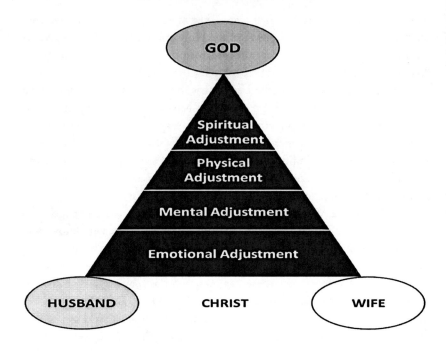

Figure 1.1. The Triangle of Marriage.

One defining principle is crucial to understand. It is through the foundation of Christ that the couple can truly adjust to one another. "Unless the Lord builds the house, they labor in vain that build it . . . " (Psalm 127:1, NKJV). It is not only crucial to the foundation of the marriage but also essential to the direction of the marriage. Joshua's proclamation is just as relevant today as it was thousands of years ago. He said to the children of Israel, " . . . choose for yourselves this day whom you will serve . . . . But as for me and my house, we will serve the Lord" (Joshua 24:15, NKJV). The last thing that a man or woman needs in their marriage is a carbon copy of themselves but this is the very step that many take after they say "I do." Scripture, in regard to the church states, "We have many members but one body; but all members do not have the same function" (Romans 12:4, NKJV). If this is an important principle in the growth and life of the church, how much more important is it in the life of families that make up the church.

A Christ-like attitude is a vital element that opens the door for personal and marital changes. Each spouse must develop an "attitude of gratitude toward the other" rather than a self-centered gratification. One can see in figure two the flow of the marriage triangle in reference to growth to God and each other. Growth flows from the emotions to the mental to the physical. The last is the spiritual adjustment, but this is the most crucial piece of the triangle. If a husband were to take out the other sections and put them aside, he would not have a complete triangle. The spiritual relationship, if taken out, will stand alone and still complete the picture of marriage. With Christ as the foundation of the marriage relationship, the adjustments flow naturally upward toward a rich and full spiritual life as seen in *figure 1.2*.

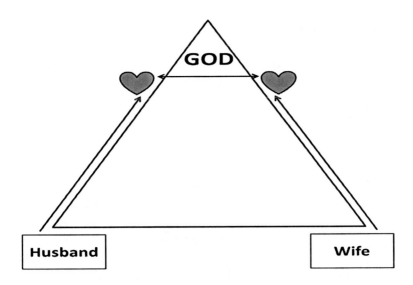

Figure 1.2. Spiritual Triangle of Marriage.

This diagram is a strong visual affirmation that the closer the couple draws to God in their walk and life of marriage, the closer they will draw to each other. This is crucial in a strong and lasting relationship. "Many of us enter into marriage with the wrong belief that our mate should be the source of all our satisfaction .... Husbands and wives can be tremendous sources of help and encouragement to each other, but if they expect to be the source of each other's happiness, disappointment looms just around the corner."[48] As we see in *figure 1.3*, God is not an intrusion in the lives of the couple but should be the very apex of life that aids the spouses to love Him and each other. Contrary to Barna's research, couples that have a real desire to know Christ individually will have a stronger tendency to love the other spouse intentionally. This powerful 'oneness' is a principle, not a social norm. Genesis 2:25, "The two of them, man and his wife, were naked but they felt no shame" (The Message) demonstrates that spouses can experience a deep level of acceptance and freedom with each other. How was this possible for Adam and Eve? "They were safe and secure with each other because they were secure in their relationship with God."[49] The main reason for this statement is that God's principles of loving Him and loving others are permanent and not socially situational. Whereas emotions will change, mental ideas will sway, and beauty will fade, the fire of passion that comes through the love of God to His children will not. Therefore, the love that flows to the spouse from God to both the husband and the wife will keep the seal of "I do!" permanent. In Titus 2:1-5, Eph. 5:25-29, and 1 Peter 3:1-7, couples come to understand that these scriptures focus on the husband loving the wife. Why is the focus on the husband? It is easier for a wife to submit to a man when she knows that he loves her and is looking out for her well-being. This type of love facilitates two important concepts.

The first concept is absolute permanency. If a person is willing to lay down his very life for someone, the expression is not one of frivolous affection but of deep, undying devotion. As Christ suffered the hardships of the cross, the beatings, the mocking, the verbal and physical abuse, His love for the Bride, the church, was unwavering and permanent, even to the point of an agonizing death on a cross. It is a blood covenant of permanence, not a contract of convenience. The second concept is absolute completeness. The bases for such expressions of love and for the teaching of them are located in passages such as Genesis 2:24 and Ephesians 5:31. These scriptures remind couples of the uniqueness of this new family structure. If the man leaves his biological family and cleaves to his wife as "one flesh," then for the man to love his wife is to love the one who has become a part of himself. The way this love flows to each spouse depends on the reservoir of self-love and respect the husband or wife has for himself or herself.

SELF ESTEEM

By far, one of the greatest areas of conflict in both youth and adults derives from having wrong attitudes about themselves. According to the Advanced Training Institute, after a period of being rejected by others, a person begins to feel as though everybody rejects him. Then he begins to reject himself. The ultimate in self-rejection is the act of suicide. In the midst of this thick cloud of despair, he has a hard time realizing that God accepts him. He, therefore, rejects God and develops a poor concept of God.[50] This can lead to an attitude of bitterness, mistrust, and resentment toward God and others. Matthew McKay writes, "Judging and rejecting yourself causes enormous pain. . . . You make it more difficult for yourself to meet people, interview for a job, or push hard for something where you might not succeed."[51] Sometimes Christians who experience this type of rejection will try to gain approval from God by a life of over-service, always trying to win God's favor. A person can have a misconception of God at this point, believing that He is a disapproving Father, waiting to chastise us when we make a mistake. "It is very hard to love God or our neighbor unless we see ourselves and others as He sees us."[52]

This harsh view of God greatly impacts the personal relationship of the husband and the wife. In marriage, some may protect themselves from rejection by avoidance, lack of communication, seeking approval through performance, and keeping others emotionally distant. "To break the cycle of self-rejection one must seek the promises from God's word rather than the positions of the world."[53] Paul states, "For we dare not class ourselves or compare ourselves with those that commend themselves. But they, measuring themselves with themselves and comparing themselves among themselves, are not wise" (2 Corinthians 10:12, NKJV). God desires for both the husband and the wife to gain their worth and value not through the spouse but through His promises in scripture. The Psalmist wrote, "I will praise you for I am fearfully and wonderfully made; marvelous are your works, and that my soul knows very well" (Psalms 139:14, NKJV).

> Thine hands have made me and fashioned me together round about; . . . Remember, I beseech thee, that thou hast made me as the clay; and wilt thou bring me into dust again? Hast thou not poured me out as milk, and curdled me like cheese? Thou hast clothed me with skin and flesh, and hast fenced me with bones and sinews. Thou hast granted me life and favor, and thy visitation hath preserved my spirit (Job 10:8-12, KJV).

Paul also exclaims, "We are His workmanship, created in Christ Jesus for His good work" (Ephesians 2:10, NKJV). Peter taught, "But ye are a chosen generation, a royal priesthood, a holy nation, a peculiar people; that ye should show forth the praises of him who hath called you out of darkness into his marvelous light" (1 Peter 2:9, KJV).

High self esteem is not a noisy conceit. It is a high sense of self-respect, a feeling of self-worth. When spouses have this understanding deep inside, they are glad to be who they are. Conceit is but whitewash to cover a low self-worth. With high self-esteem, one does not waste time and energy impressing others to feel valuable. This is also important when husbands and wives become parents. Self-esteem in our children is the "mainspring" that slates every child for success or failure as a human being. The result of this is often experienced though the visual relationship of the parents. It is through studying God's Word and living a godly life that spouses, children and the world witness what it means to be a disciple of Christ.

Christians are not the same as people of the world. Therefore, Christian marriages should not be the same as non-Christian marriages. This has been the scriptural position since the beginning of the New Testament church. Paul writes in 1 Thessalonians 4:4-5, ". . . each of you should learn to control his own body in a way that is holy and honorable, not in passionate lust like the heathen, who do not know God". Our marital relationships are holy and they are holy because of the Christian commitments couples are willing to make. 2 Peter 1:10-11 helps spouses to begin a foundation of this discipleship process. In verse 10, the Apostle Peter challenged his first-century readers to confirm their "calling and election" of God. Using a legal and commercial analogy, Peter challenged them to present to the world the "proof of purchase" of their union with Christ. The Holman CSB translates a portion of 2 Peter 1:10 as "make every effort to confirm your calling and election." The King James Version renders these same words as "make your calling and election sure." The Greek word for "confirm" or "sure" originally meant "standing firm on the feet" and then came to mean "steady, "certain," or "firm." In ancient transactions this term was used to describe what a seller would give a buyer as confirmation of the sale. The buyer could then present this confirmation to a third party as proof of purchase. Thus the word is a legal term to indicate something is valid.

Christian couples demonstrate, by their continual growth in Christ and consistent lives, confirmation of their salvation. One does not, by consistent Christian living and spiritual growth, earn salvation, but demonstrates the validity of his confession of faith in these ways. Before someone can confirm that salvation, one must first encounter the living Christ and call on Him as Savior. To use an old baseball analogy, one needs to go to first base first before he or she can go onto the last three. If a person does not know Christ as his or her Savior, the rest is *work* and not *worship*. God's Word in a couple's life gives the confidence to know that they are saved and not just hope they are saved. Some will come to the altar and talk to a minister about rededicating their lives to Christ. Whereas this may be a great first step in turning your life around if you are a Christian, it is a wasted step if you has never asked Christ to come into the heart. It is in a complete commitment to Christ that a husband and wife can accept and live out the godly responsibilities in the marriage.

GODLY RESPONSIBILITIES

Many Christians are more concerned about their personality than their character. Worse yet, I fear that some confuse or equate the two. Some women tend to think that the ideal husband and spiritual leader is the one with the 'salesman-type' personality; he is outgoing, aggressive, and assertive. Some women who are married to men who have a less aggressive nature are tempted to look down on their husbands because they are not domineering enough. These wives should talk to some of the women who have the assertive husbands. Some men think that the ideal 'submissive' wife is the woman who is shy and passive. In both cases, personality has been confused with character. God is not nearly as concerned with our personality as He is with our character. Aggressive men are not necessarily better leaders, and certainly they may not be more godly leaders, nor are passive women necessarily more submissive.[54]

Regarding the true foundation of a husband's and wife's responsibility toward God and each other, the Bible states, "Nevertheless let each one of you in particular so love his own wife as himself and let the wife see that she respects her husband" (Ephesians 5:33, NKJV). "However, it is only when the principles concerning marriage are understood the way God intended them — not the way society has interpreted them — that husbands and wives can find true confidence and freedom in their roles and God-given joy in their union." [55] Christian couples that apply biblical principles of God's holiness to their marriage can develop a stronger foundation than those of unbelieving friends and neighbors. "God counsels not only that we may have eternal life, but comfort here and now. A godly marriage is a bit of heaven on earth."[56] In marriage, holiness is anything but boring. It is the kind of purity and trustworthiness from which the deepest passions of love and respect flow.[57] These two duties, love and respect, are mentioned particularly because they are the most common failures in marriage. "Five out of ten marriages today are ending in divorce because love alone is not enough. Yes, love is vital, especially for the wife, but what we have missed is the husband's need for respect."[58] Henry Cloud writes, "The law of respect fosters love. Loving your mate means desiring and protecting his or her freedom of choice."[59]

Any man that hopes to be a godly husband will find it necessary to understand what it means to be a man of courage who fears the Lord. He must also be committed to the goal of personal holiness. What is holiness to the husband? Bob Lepine writes:

> If he's not first and foremost a godly man, he will never be the kind of husband that God has called him to be. His respect and reverance for the One who has bought his life back from the slave market of sin should provide the drive and determination to live his newly redeemed life in a way that honors his Creator.[60]

> This is also true for the wife. Although different in her position in marriage, she is directly responsible for her actions, attitude, and honor toward God in her relationship with her husband.

In 1 Timothy 3:8 Paul explains four attributes of the husband. Although this is used often as the text for a deacon's ordination, it is a clear understanding of the qualities that God set forth in the life of a Christian leader. The godly husband is reverent, not double-tongued, not given to much wine, and not greedy for money. To have a happy marriage, it is necessary for the husband to take the lead spiritually. Reverence for God displayed in the family will help overcome many challenges in the married life. Prayer will also give needed strength for those difficult times.

A husband's love is the foundation of all other duties toward his wife. Everything flows from this. Without love, every performance of duty toward her seems hard. The love of a husband to his wife is peculiar to this relationship. Paul writes, "Husbands, love your wives just as Christ also loved the church. . ." (Ephesians 5:25, NKJV). While men cannot attain equality with Christ, yet the quality of their love should be the same as His. How, then, does Jesus Christ love His church? "His love was so real and intense that He died for the church. It was free, without conditions before or expectations after. Jesus gave Himself to cleanse His church, implying she was no beauty beforehand. The husband must draw love from his wife by his own love. True love is more about bettering the object loved than enriching the subject."[61] Christ loved the church "that He might sanctify and cleanse her with the washing of water by the word" (Ephesians 5:26, NKJV). This teaches the husband to labor diligently to further the sanctification of his wife. "So husbands ought to love their wives as their own bodies. He who loves his wife, loves himself" (Ephesians 5:28, NKJV). "Therefore, let each one of you in particular so love his own wife as himself . . . ." (Ephesians 5:33, NKJV). Now although this pattern is less than Christ's love for His church, it is easier to comprehend. One will handle his own sores and grief more tenderly than anyone else. "No one ever hated his own flesh, but nourishes and cherishes it" (Ephesians 5:29, NKJV). Wives are like crystal glasses, easily broken if not tenderly handled.

The wife's respect for her husband is just as foundational in the growth of a marriage as is the love from the husband to his wife. Paul lists four attributes for the godly wife in 1Timothy 3:11. She is reverent, not given to slander, temperate, and faithful in all things. Just as the husband needs to seek God daily, so does the wife. It takes two people to make a good marriage. To make it a great marriage, it takes three: husband, wife, and God. Paul calls on the wives to be temperate, which means to be moderate or steady in all things. It is easy to jump from one extreme to the other. This will only add confusion and turmoil in the marriage. Finally, Paul calls on the wife to be a faithful wife. A marriage is built on trust, so being faithful in all things is an essential. Although important for both spouses, this is her special qualification. If she has beauty and wisdom but no respect for her husband, she will negatively impact the marriage. Creation suggests it. She was made after the man (1 Timothy 2:13), from the man (1 Corinthians 11:8), and for the man (1 Corinthians 11:9). This order was not by man's doing, but God's. Even after the fall, the divine order stands; " . . . he shall rule over you" (Genesis 3:16, NKJV). The New Testament confirms all this in Colossians 3:18 and 1 Peter 3:1-6. In the Old Testament, it states, "All wives will honor their husbands, both great and small" (Esther 1:20, NKJV). A wife should ponder the excellence of her husband, and value him properly. If he is not accomplished, then she should consider the excellence of his place as "the image and glory of God" (1 Corinthians 11:7, NKJV).

Being a godly spouse is such a big challenge that couples must prepare for it beforehand. Richard Steele notes,

> An upright heart is needed to keep these commandments of God. An upright heart will choose the safest course, even if it is the hardest. It will suffer the worst injury rather than cause the least. It will watch against the beginnings of sin, which produce marriage's worst troubles. The upright husband and wife will strive each to do their own duty, and will be most severe against their own failures.[62]

Dennis Rainey states in his book, *Preparing for Marriage,*

> No other human relationship can approach the potential for intimacy and closeness than can be found within the matrimony walls. Yet, no other relationship can have the incredible number of adjustments and potential hurts and disappointments. "There is no way to avoid difficulties in marriage . . . . But there is much you can do to prepare for it."[63]

HOME

Psychologist Norman Wright expressed, ". . . within each of us is the hunger for contact, acceptance, belonging, intimate exchange, responsiveness, support, love and the touch of tenderness."[64] In marriage a caring partner can fill that need so a man or woman does not have to feel lonely. God planned it that way when he created Adam. Genesis 2:18 states, "It is not good that the man should be alone; I will make a helper comparable to him" (NKJV). Simply stated, God made Adam a companion suited for him. Neither a beautiful environment nor a variety of animals would fill the need in Adam's life. Marriage, right from the start, is to be a relationship based on mutual, caring companionship. It is not a dictator or doormat style relationship. Paul makes this clear when he says husband and wife relationships require "submitting yourselves one to another .

. ." (Ephesians 5:21, NKJV). Couples who want to keep the home fires burning will make time for each other and that time will be quality time.

In the building of a Christian family there are two areas to consider. First, one needs to know about the foundation upon which to build. Second, one must be concerned about the materials with which to build. What is the only foundation upon which a home, a family, can stand? What are the foundations upon which you build? Jesus Christ, in Matthew 7, said that there are only two possible foundations. One either builds his family-life upon the sand, refusing to subject oneself to the Word of Jesus Christ; or one builds upon the rock of the Word of God. "Therefore, whoever hears these sayings of mine, and does them," Jesus said, "I will liken to a wise man who built his house on the rock" (Matthew 7:24, NKJV). Therefore, the only foundation for building a Christian home is on the Word of God. Anything else is sand. "If you build your idea of a family upon rationalism you are building upon sand. That is, if you make up your own mind, or if you consider current popular opinion to be the final bar of judgment, if you are building upon that, you are building upon sand." [65]

A Christian couple's conviction must be that whatever God has said is absolute and final because God is absolute and final. We must go about the building of a Christian home with the conviction that II Timothy 3:16 is true, namely, that all Scripture is given by inspiration of God and is, therefore, "profitable for doctrine, for reproof, for correction, for instruction in righteousness, that the man of God may be complete, and thoroughly equipped for every good work" (II Timothy 3:16-17, NKJV). A godly husband and wife must not take their principles for family living from their own heads, from society, not even from tradition, but from God and His Scriptures. Everything in the Christian home must be built upon the foundation of God's Word. Why should children obey their parents? Why should husbands love their wives? There is no satisfactory answer other than what God's Word sets forth as the foundational standard.

Second, when a couple builds a Christian home, they must also focus on the material used in construction. The materials with which couples build a Christian home are those biblical principles that spouses must elicit and draw forth from the Bible in an intelligent manner. That means that both husband and wife know them in their minds and out of believing hearts seek to put those principles into practice in their family life. "A biblical worldview is based on the infallible Word of God. When you believe the Bible is entirely true, it is the foundation of everything you say and do." [66] If a young husband and wife are deeply committed to Jesus Christ and to each other, they can enjoy enormous advantages within marriage.

A meaningful prayer life is an important ingredient in maintaining a Christ-centered home. Of course, some people use prayer the way they follow their horoscopes, attempting to manipulate an unidentified "higher power" around them. It is impossible to overstate the need for prayer in the fabric of family life. A personal relationship with Jesus Christ is the cornerstone of marriage, giving meaning and purpose to every dimension of living. According to an article in the 2000 winter edition of *Newsweek*, "81 percent of mothers and 78 percent of fathers say they plan eventually to send their young child to Sunday school or some other type of religious training."[67] There are many parents that want to raise their child with an understanding of right and wrong but "prayerful parenting goes even deeper than instilling moral values. Prayerful parents provide a spiritual underpinning to their kid's lives . . . ."[68] Being able to bow in prayer as the day begins or ends gives expression to the frustrations and concerns that might not otherwise be ventilated. On the other end of that prayer line is a loving heavenly Father who has promised to hear and answer a couple's petitions for their home. A question that needs to be settled in the lives of the Christian parent is, "Do you practice the presence of God in prayer in front of your children?" John Drescher wrote, "Religious words have no value to the child only as experience in the home gives them meaning."[69] In this day of disintegrating families, Christian husbands and wives dare not try to make it on their own. To do this would risk the greatest treasures that a couple can have, their children.

CHILDREN

Christian parents face the difficult task of raising children in a world of shifting ethics, vague moral absolutes, and increasing social issues. It seems that children in the past grew up in a Mayberry-type society that clearly defined what was right and what was wrong. Even in the old show, *Leave It To Beaver*, parents were recognized as the primary authority figure in their children's lives. Now, our children conform to the growing immorality, anti-family, and anti-parent concepts in schools and media. Author Foster Cline expressed regarding the challenges in parenting, "I can't understand it. It worked for my dad!" This may echo the thoughts of many parents. The internet explosion, the human rights revolution, cell phones and changes in the nuclear family have radically changed how children view life.[70] Regarding the previous *Newsweek* article, it is comforting to know that many parents want to raise children that are empathic, know right from wrong, and attempt to follow the Golden Rule. But what are the prevailing messages in today's books, movies, and on TV?

Parents show increasing concern as their children are encouraged to shun strict rules and biblical truths. Whenever the application of God's laws is mentioned, flurries of organizations warn parents not to impose their own values upon their children. The Christian parent understands the wickedness of exchanging God's truth for a lie.[71]

The Bible speaks of the "backbiters, haters of God, violent, proud, boasters, inventors of evil things; disobedient to parents" (Romans 1:30, NKJV). Rebellion and disobedience are just as pervasive today as parental authority disintegrates. Parents must choose who and what shapes their children's lives. Without a doubt, God still holds parents responsible to instruct and to discipline their children.

Building a strong, loving family in today's culture takes determination and a conscious effort on the part of every family member. Michael Levine stated, "Having children makes you no more a parent than having a piano makes you a pianist."[72] With so many things competing for our time and attention it is easy to lose sight of the value and significance of the close, loving relationships our families can provide. When a person comes to the end of his life, he realizes that the only things that really mattered were the loving relationships established and cultivated throughout the years. During the first five or six years of a child's life, he or she is impacted by the home environment. "As we grow up, we tend to adopt the ways of thinking of everyone around us . . . . We simply pick up the thinking patterns of those in our environment."[73] Parents are the educators who teach the child to listen, to talk, and to understand the meanings of words. Parents help their child explore and begin to understand the world, and guide him as he interprets the information he learns every day. "In a real sense, parents are the models a child imitates and this child mirrors adult gestures and way of walking."[74] Matthew McKay writes, "As they grow older, children will have other mirrors that show them who they are. Teachers, friends, . . . but a child will return to the reflection in the mirror that his parents held for this sense of goodness, importance, and basic worth."[75] This mirroring may also apply to a parent's walk of faith. "Train up a child in the way he should go" (Proverb 22:6, NKJV) is not only a command from the Lord in a parent's teaching but also a directive in how that parent lives in front of their children.

Children imitate the way in which adults speak and thereby reflect positive or negative home ideas and values. "The basics of biblical parenting involve more than simply raising a child. Parents are directly responsible to God for more than providing food, shelter, and protection. When we adopt God's standards as our own, we produce quality character that is different from a child's natural inclinations."[76] Marriage is the mold that shapes our children's most basic understanding of themselves. Les Parrot in his book, *The Parent You Want to Be*, writes: "Your child's character hinges on the traits you exhibit as a parent. Who you are as a parent isn't left to fate, luck, or chance. You can choose to be the kind of parent you want to be."[77] Role and gender confusion, trauma, and a dysfunctional environment in these formative years can have negative consequences in a child's self-identity for a lifetime. Regarding these impacts, Laura Schlessinger writes, "I believe that many people don't even realize that their childhood history has impacted their adult thought and behavior"[78] Therefore, a biblical perspective on what it means to be a man and a woman as well as a dad and mom demonstrated through the lives of the parent, is an important dynamic to a child's growth. A parent shapes a child's attitudes, actions, and associations. When moms and dads are inconsistent in delivering godly instruction and wisdom to their children, they practice ineffective biblical parenting. When a dad places unreasonable demands by abusing his authority, he practices ineffective biblical parenting. When both mom and dad make anything more important than the children, they take another step away from love, and a step away from effective biblical parenting. In a recent *Focus on the Family* survey, spiritual training was reported as one of the top three issues with which parents need help. Building a spiritual heritage takes a bit of planning, effort, and creativity, but the most important thing is to make it meaningful.

Creating special, teachable moments with children is a precious, yet difficult, responsibility. Parents can capture moments throughout the day to teach and impress biblical principles on their children. If a couple's home is filled with tension and chaos, it will be difficult for spiritual values to be taught or caught. However, if the home environment is sweet and restful, it's more fertile ground for spiritual training. Family traditions are a powerful way to impress on your children the power of family togetherness. Whether the dad or mom passed down stories, beliefs and/or customs, traditions can help parents establish a special identity for the family.[79]

Parental instruction is an arduous journey that begins at birth and continues for a lifetime. There may also be countless times when our children make careless decisions and even choose to reject instruction. These are the times when discipline is most necessary. Theories on correct discipline change every few years; however, the Bible never changes. If children do not obey, they must receive correction. The Bible teaches that a rod of correction does this. "The rod and rebuke give wisdom, but a child left to himself brings shame to his mother" (Proverbs 29:15, NKJV). "Often parents become weary disciplining young children. At times, a typical day seems to consist of nagging and scolding. Parents wonder if they have ruined every chance for a loving relationship with their children. They may even be tempted to give up altogether."[80] God entrusts children to the parents' specific care. He wants each mother and father to know that kind, firm correction will train their children to obey Him. "Children, obey your parents in all things, for this well pleasing to the Lord" (Colossians 3:20, NKJV). Consistent, loving correction helps children learn biblical truths like self-discipline. By applying God's standards, fathers and mothers can also receive God's blessings as parents. In these blessings, couples must become good stewards for their family and finances.

FINANCES

Financial planner Dave Ramsey sited *Worth* magazine and *USA Today*'s surveys regarding conflict over money. He writes, ". . . the results of a study done for the Lutheran Brotherhood shows that when we fight about money we fight most about the use of credit, shopping, and spending . . . ."[81] A *Jet Magazine* article, "Why Money is the Leading Cause of Divorce," reported a study conducted by Citibank showing that 57 percent of divorces are caused by money problems and *The Detroit News* expressed statistics of 70 percent.[82] When I counsel couples regarding finances in marriage, one principle I state is that money should always be kept in your hand and not in your heart. Jesus knew this when He said, "Take heed, and beware of covetousness, for a man's life consisteth not in the abundance of the things which he possesseth" (Luke 12:15, KJV). Paul knew how dangerous the love of money was when he said, "But Godliness with contentment is great gain. For we brought nothing into this world, and we can take nothing out of it. But if we have food and clothing, we will be content with that . . . . For the love of money is a root of all kinds of evil" (I Timothy 6:6-8, 10). According to Bill Bachrach, most financial planning starts with an assessment of goals. Bachrach explains, "Important as these are, they do not provide you with the big picture, the 'why' behind the rest of the plan, your values. Goals are tangible results you seek, while values are the intangibles that make pursuit of those goals genuinely meaningful to you."[83]

In a marriage, there is no 'my money' and 'your money' or 'my debts' and 'your debts.' There is only our money and our debts. A couple cannot be one if they separate their lives by separating their finances. God brings a couple closer if, from the very beginning, they establish God's Word as their financial guide and then follow those principles. A marriage is not a 50/50 relationship, as many people think. It is a 95/5 relationship on both sides. Each must be willing to yield 95 percent of their rights to their spouses. If they are not willing to do that, it will not work.[84]

No viable marriage can survive a "his or her" relationship for long, because it is totally contrary to God's plan. Couples should avoid having separate financial anything, including checking accounts, because when they develop a his money/ her money philosophy, it can lead to a him-versus-her mentality. Unwillingness to join all assets and bank accounts after marriage is perhaps a danger signal that unresolved trust issues could still be lingering or developing in the relationship. During pre-marriage counseling, I asked a couple about their financial plan regarding the checkbook. Quickly they responded that there would be two checking accounts, his and hers. I asked why they were approaching their finances this way. They explained that in the event of a divorce, it would be easier to settle the financial issues. The look on my face was one of disbelief. I then asked the couple if they were preparing for marriage or the future divorce. The couple, as they pondered the implications of their quick decision, was silent. A husband's and wife's income in marriage should be merged and shared. Someone should be in charge of keeping a budget for the household, and whatever funds there are should be held mutually. This will require a lot of faith in the Lord, as well as in your spouse.[85]

The key to understanding God's will in finances is the proper understanding of the word stewardship. By the Merriam-Webster definition, a steward is "One actively concerned with the direction of the affairs of and organization."[86] God says that if we pray for anything in His will, believing, it will be given to us. However, God's will and His ways do not always coincide with ours. So, when we turn our finances over to God, we also must be willing to accept His direction. Too often we impatiently seek our own way without any clear direction from Him, sometimes even borrowing money to do His work. We forget that God says He will not frustrate His work for the lack of money (see Luke 22:35).[87] The Christian couple is merely a steward of God's property while they live on earth. God can choose to entrust them with little or much as He desires, but in no case do we ever take ownership. Larry Burkett explains, If Christians can accept that role of stewards and manage God's resources according to His direction, God will continue to entrust them with even more . . . . Moreover, until the Christian acknowledges God's total ownership, he cannot experience God's direction in financial management.

Jesus told a parable about a householder giving his servants talents in Matthew 25:14-30. The amount was different with each person. One servant received five talents, another servant two, while the last servant only received one. Each of these servants then chose how they managed the master's resources that had been entrusted to them while he was away. When the master of the house came back each of the servants gave an account of how they managed their master's talents. The indication here is that two of these men either possessed good stewardship skills, or they sought the benefit of financial counseling. The one with one talent did not do well at all. He did not lose what he had but did not gain from it either.[88] There is a concept in the parable of Matthew 25 that seems foreign to the world's way of reckoning. The talents did not belong to the servants but rather to the master, and they were just managing those talents until that master returned. One truth that is gleaned from this parable is that everything spouses have in this life has been given to them from God to manage. Couples have a choice in how they manage what has been given, and it is only common sense that they should learn good stewardship practices through financial counseling.[89]

Stewardship, therefore, is inherent to an understanding of wise money management. That means that money is a means to a goal while not being the goal itself. The principle taught in Proverbs 6:6-8 is one suited to every couple's understanding of faithful financial living. It states, "Go to the ant, O sluggard, observe her ways and be wise, which having no chief, officer, or ruler, prepares her food in the summer and gathers her provision in the harvest" (NASV). Larry Burkett also writes,

> Many Christians mistakenly believe that accumulating a surplus is somehow unspiritual. It may be, if the attitude is one of hoarding. Hoarding means that the goal is to create a surplus. In contrast, saving is anticipating a future financial need and preparing for it.[90]

Within a marriage relationship the husband and wife are partners who are dedicated to one another. A bond of uncompromising devotion creates a healthy atmosphere for togetherness: studying God's Word, praying, and even managing money. Just as it takes two to make a marriage successful, it takes two to establish a clear line of communication in financial planning.
The Invested Year

The organ plays the wedding theme and the newly married man and woman exit through the church doors. Their whole life as a husband and wife is in front of them. There will be many decisions to make, experiences to have, and journeys to take. They will face important questions in their new life together. One question of great importance is not where they will live but how they live. It is not what career they will have but how they will worship together. It will not be what investments to make in mutal bonds but what investments they will make in their marriage. Contrary to Barna's survey of marriage, it is this researcher's conviction that for the Christian marriage to stand the test of time, the foundation of Christ and a personal acceptance of a covenant commitment to marriage is what will protect the marriage year by year. Barna's study does explain an important truth in the marriage relationship. There are important principles that if a couple violates, regardless of faith, can lead to disaster. As an example, we live by the law of gravity. One can argue against it and say he does not believe in it but if he jumps off of a building, he will feel the impact of his mistake. To take the analogy further, if you are a Christian driving toward a curve at 70 miles per hour and do not slow down, you will go over the edge. Even if you have an "I love Jesus" bumper sticker and are listening to Gospel music, you are still violating the law of gravity and you will fall. This is also true for the principles of marriage. These eight principles will protect and provide for the couple as they take the time to look inward in their hearts (Temperaments, Adjustments) upward to their creator (self-Image, Discipleship, Responsibilities), and outward to their world (Home, Children, Finances). "Many couples wonder how the blending of two personalities and sets of ambitions, desires, and dreams could ever be expected by a wise and all-knowing God! Trying to adjust from freedom to partnership can be difficult and exasperating but it's a process, not just a destination."[91] It is in the practice of these eight marriage-enhancing principles that a family will thrive and survive the daily storms of life.

CHAPTER TWO

BASIC COUPLE TRAINING

THE CONFIGURATIONS AND CONNECTIONS

During the beginning weeks of the Basic Combat Training phase, a table packed with radios, rolls of wire, and tools was placed in front of me. I, as a new soldier, received instructions regarding the set-up, maintenance, and trouble-shooting of the Army field radio. While the Drill Sergeant explained the importance of correct wiring, my mind drifted back home. While growing up, my father and brother talked at great lengths about electrical stuff, Ohm's Law and the importance of proper wiring. My only electrical interest was if the television came on when I pushed the button (not the remote). After this training, I gained a much needed respect for circuits, wiring, and electrical equipment. I slowly and carefully took the field phones apart to avoid experiencing the feeling of being "bit" by an electrical current. I also learned the consequences of improper procedures and half-hearted attention.

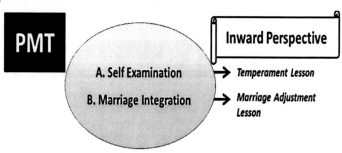

As couples enter into their Basic Marriage Training (BMT) phase, they discover a new, more important law of electrical configurations and connection. It is not Ohm's Law but the "I Do" law. It is in this relationship law that the true sparks can and will fly. For example, why is it when you think you know someone, he or she does something that zaps you like a wrongly wired field phone? It is amazing that after a man says "I do!", the simple things that were celebrated as fun and unique about him are now the very things that make his wife want to strangle him. Welcome to the world of configurations and connections, or as they are called in marriage, temperaments and adjustments. The apostle Paul expressed a conflict between flesh and faith when he wrote,

> To will is present with me, but how to perform what is good I do not find. For the good that I will to do, I do not do; but the evil I will not to do, that I practice. Now if I do what I will not to do, it is no longer I who do it, but sin that dwells in me. (Rom. 7:18-20, NKJV).

Tim LaHaye, author of Spirit-Controlled Temperament, explains this passage as it relates to temperaments. LaHaye writes,

> Note that Paul differentiated between himself and that uncontrollable force within by saying; It is no longer I who do it, but sin that dwells in me. The 'I' is Paul's person; soul, will, and human mind. The sin that resided in him resulted from the natural weaknesses that he, like all human beings, received from his parents. At the moment of our conception we all inherited a basic genetic temperament that contains both our strengths and our weaknesses. This temperament is called several things in the Bible: the natural man, the flesh, the old man, and corruptible flesh, to name a few. It is the basic impulse of our being that seeks to satisfy our wants.[92]

Temperaments within the marriage relationship are like the internal configurations that cause us to act and react in certain ways. The marriage adjustments are the external connections that allow us to 'plug and play' the life changing game of marriage with one's spouse. First, couples should examine the internal configurations of self and spouse.

INTERNAL CONFIGURATIONS
The Inspection of Supplies and Examination of Self

To successfully hook up an Army field radio, soldiers must take the time to inspect the supplies, especially the wires. They also need a comprehensive understanding as to what each wire will do when connected to the phone. Not inspecting the wires or knowing the unique qualities of each leads to a faulty hook up. This can cause a short to occur and damage the phone, soldier, or both. So too must couples take the time to inspect and understand the wires that complete the "circuit of self." David Keirsey identified three primary wires that generate a total connection to the internal man and woman in marriage. The three primary wires are *temperament, character,* and *personality*. Regarding these three wires, he writes that "we are predisposed to develop certain attitudes . . . and certain actions but that these actions are unified — they hang together."[93]

THREE PRIMARY WIRES

First, the *temperament* wire is the combination of inborn traits that subconsciously affects all behavior. It could be described as the black grounding wire. Florence Littauer expressed, "We started out with a combination of ingredients that made us different from our brothers and sisters."[94] These traits, which are passed on by genetics, are based on hereditary factors and arranged at the time of conception. Six people contribute through the gene pool to the makeup of every baby: two parents and four grandparents. Some authorities suggest that we may get more genes from our grandparents than our parents. That could account for the greater resemblance of some children to their grandparents than to their parents. The alignment of temperament traits, though unseen, is just as predictable as the color of eyes, hair, or size of body.[95] Keirsey described these traits as "inborn and unified."[96] It is these traits that make one either extrovert (outgoing) or introvert (reserved). An example of this is the birth of identical twins. Although they may look alike, their temperaments can be worlds apart.

The second wire is that of *character*. This wire combines temperament, training, moral values, beliefs, and habit patterns. It is indeed the net result of all the influences and religious commitment in life. One pastor stated, "Character is your hidden self when no one is looking!" LaHaye explains character as "the result of your natural temperament modified by childhood training, education, and basic attitudes, beliefs, principles, and motivations. It is sometimes referred to as 'the soul' of a person, which is made up of the mind, emotions, and will."[97] In his book, *The 21 Irrefutable Laws of Leadership,* John Maxwell quotes General Norman Schwarzkopf, "Leadership is a potent combination of strategy and character. But if you must be without one, be without strategy."[98] Character is what makes trust possible in any relationship, especially marriage.

The final wire is personality. Personality is the outward expression, which may or may not be the same as a person's character, depending on how genuine that person is. Personality can be a pleasing facade for an unpleasant or weak character. "Many people go through life acting a part on the basis of what they think they should be, or how they want people to see them, rather than as they really are. This is a formula for mental and spiritual chaos. It is caused by following the human formula which places an emphasis on the externals."[99] Littauer labeled these responses as "masks of survival."[100] The Bible tells us, "Man looks at the outward appearance, but the Lord looks at the heart" (1 Sam. 16:7, NKJV) and, "Out of it [the heart] spring the issues of life" (Prov. 4:23, NKJV). The place to change behavior is inside each of us, not outside. LaHaye reminds us "some Christians erroneously think that their temperaments have changed, but that is impossible. As we have seen, we are born with them. The Holy Spirit can, however, modify our temperaments so they appear to have changed."[101]

THE IMPORTANCE OF THE WIRING DIAGRAM

When couples finally understand the wires, they often ask, "Now what do we do with these wires?" Essential piece to completing an electrical job is the wiring diagram. This crucial piece of paper aids a person in learning the value of proper results. Why is this area so important for a marriage? Today's research shows the primary cause of divorce is personality differences. In the 1990's the main causes of conflict/divorce were either finances or communication. In the 2000's our personality differences cause the *rub instead of the love*. By looking at the divorce graph in *figure2.2*, one will see that the two primary "killers" of the marriage relationship are *infidelity* and *clash of character*. As stated in a 2006 research paper, "Incompatibility of characters shows that nearly four in ten divorced persons report infidelity or incompatibility of characters was the reason for their marriage breakdown. An equal amount of men and women identify these reasons as the cause of marital dissolution."[102] Often, couples go into the relationship with expectations of finding a carbon copy. This is typically expressed with the words, "We have so much in common." It is important to have some common ground and similarities in likes and dis-likes. Conflict comes, however, when one spouse is trying to make the other spouse like him. This can cause aggravation, frustration, and a feeling of devaluation within the relationship. During a marriage conference, I exclaimed, "If it were not for the differences between my wife and me, I would have ended up on the street with a cardboard sign reading, *Will Preach for Food*! I am thankful my wife's ability to do math and keep the checkbook is greatly different from my own. I round up to the nearest dollar and she balances the check-book to the penny."

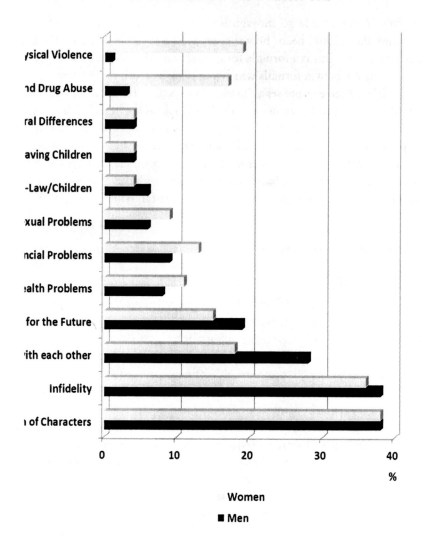

Figure 2.2 Divorce Graph

UNCOVERING THE WIRING DIAGRAM

In the first part of the century, a good many writers essayed their views on temperament. Four of these, Erich Adickes, Ernst Kreschmer, Eduard Spranger, and Erich Fromm, agreed with each other in how they defined temperament and character types. These men "saw the usefulness of an ancient belief that came primarily from the Greek and Romans . . . . It was the Roman physician

Galen who, developing the ideas of Hippocrates, proposed that it was not the gods that determined what we do; rather, it is the balance of our bodily fluids, the four 'humors' as they were called."[103] During the 19th century, the thought that temperament determines character was diminished by the prevailing ideas of two men, Sigmund Freud and Ivan Pavlov. Freud "reduced mankind to mere animal . . . Pavlov reduced man to a machine . . . ."[104]

Even so, the temperament theory found new champions in Europe and America in the first half of the 20th century. Tim LaHaye expounded on the four different temperament styles of Choleric, Sanguine, Melancholy, and Phlegmatic in his book, *Why You Act the Way You Do*. Smalley and John Trent, however, took these primary temperament types and develop a different electrical wiring diagram for home life. Their use of animals to describe the temperament traits has greatly helped couples to understand the internal wiring diagram. It uncovered the natural born strengths and exposed potential weaknesses.

Smalley and Trent liken the *Choleric* to a lion. Lions are natural leaders. "Lions feel very strongly that life is a series of problems they need to solve or challenges they need to meet."[105] They are very goal oriented and have the motto, *Let's do it now!* If not careful, the choleric can push his strength to an extreme and become stubborn, manipulative and intimidating. "Lions can be so strong that they win every verbal battle but end up losing the war for their family's hearts."[106] The *Sanguine* temperament is like an Otter. Otters are a party waiting to happen. Smalley states, "If there is a way to have fun doing something, you can expect an otter to try it."[107] They enjoy being the center of attention but can fear rejection. According to Littauer, "The most obvious way to spot a popular sanguine is by listening in on any group and locating the one that is talking the loudest and chatting the most. . . ."[108] This makes for the "perfect recipe for the personality that's most vulnerable to peer pressure."[109] They have the gift of gab and are tremendous motivators. Their favorite motto is; *Trust Me. It will work out!* The Golden Retriever represents the *Melancholy* temperament. Golden Retrievers are extremely loyal friends and will listen deeply to any situation and problems. "Of all the animals in the family zoo, golden retrievers can absorb the most emotional pain and still maintain their commitment to another person."[110] They are the artists and creative ones that can suffer from bouts of depression, moodiness, and indecisiveness. They also do not like change. Their motto for life is "Let's keep things the way they are!" The last temperament, *Phlegmatic,* is the Beaver. Meticulous and dedicated to quality, Beavers not only read the manuals but also write them. They can become perfectionist in approach and will often stop a project that will not turn out perfect. Since they are the people that are steadfast on facts and accuracy, their life motto is "Let's do this right"[111] It is important for Beavers to learn "that it's all right to fail and that it's healthy to call for help when they are struggling."[112] It is no wonder that our homes can become the Serengeti rather than suburbia. Couples need to understand that they are not just one temperament but a mixture of all. "We are a blend of at least two temperaments; one predominates, the other is secondary."[113]

Only when both husband and wife realize God has given someone different to complement his and her life that spouses will grow together in the marriage relationship. This is a perfect picture of lives becoming one both internally and externally through the ongoing process of marriage. There are three final thoughts to remember regarding these important temperament wires of marriage. First is self-acceptance. This concept brings people to an understanding of who they are in the framework that exposes both strengths and weaknesses, hence their own temperament style. Secondly, there is self-improvement. As one examines both strengths and weaknesses, he is better able to call upon God for His resources to improve the temperament. Lastly, there needs to be an understanding and acceptance of the others' temperaments. As long as people live, there will be confrontations of personality styles. When others try to understand why people act the way they do, it is "easier to accept and love them."[114] It first begins with knowing why our spouses act the way they do and then making the needed adjustments to them. This final thought leads to the external connections of marriage adjustments.

EXTERNAL CONNECTIONS
TEAM INTERACTION

Once soldiers learn the internal configurations for the field phone, they now work together as a team to hook everything up. The first task of the training largely depended on the individual soldier learning the equipment. The success of this second task hinges on the ability of two soldiers to work together. As a team, one will check and run the wires while the other prepares the phone for hook up. There are two important factors in this teamwork interaction. First is the communication cable. It is extremely important to have the best and not one that is old, worn out, or frayed. To use an old one will only result in static and not success. Second is the need for clean electrical connections on the phone. If the preventive maintenance was not conducted properly, the dirt, grime and sludge of the elements will block any electrical flow. Both soldiers work to inspect and re-inspect each step taken to hook up the phone. If it is left to only one set of eyes, it increases the possibility of both failing in the end.

MARRIAGE INTEGRATION

Couples must learn to work together if they want their marriage to survive the natural elements of life. As in the example above, two sets of heads and eyes are better than one set. There is continuous need for preventive maintenance of self and spouse within the marriage. In the following section are important factors both husband and wife must consider in the proper adjustment in the marriage.

THE ELECTRICAL CONNECTIONS

Have you ever turned the key in the car ignition only to hear the deafening sound of silence? This usually happened when the wind was blowing, the rain was coming down in buckets, and you needed to be somewhere thirty minutes ago. Sometimes, marriage can feel like that as well. One thinks he has kept the vehicle of matrimony well serviced only to find his marriage dead on the side of the road. Just as a car needs an electrical spark to run, couples need a special type of electrical boost in marriage that comes through a cable called attitude. Consider a historical man of energy. *Life Magazine* named him the number one man of the millennium. The number of things he invented is astounding — 1,093. He held more patents than any other person in the world, having been granted at least one every year for sixty-five consecutive years. Who is he? His name is Thomas Edison. As John Maxwell explained, the power of Edison's ability to energize the world was with his great attitude. Maxwell stated, "Most people credit Edison's work to creative genius. He credited it to hard work. 'Genius,' Edison declared, 'is ninety-nine percent perspiration and one percent inspiration.' I believe his success was also the result of a third factor; his positive attitude." [115] So if the marriage cable of attitude supplies a source of energy for the marriage, what are the electrical connections needed for successful adjustments in marriage? Consider the following four important connections.

EMOTIONAL ADJUSTMENTS

The emotional level of a relationship is where everything begins. Some may disagree with this perspective but there has to be an emotional type of connection that draws someone toward another life. It may not be the famed, "Love at first sight" but there is an instant electrical sensation that goes through the heart that makes it beat faster when spotting that perfect someone. As a young college student, I felt this when seeing my wife. I spotted her from the back of the chemistry class as she walked toward the front of the class and sat on the front row. There were three things I immediately recognized. First was that she was a knock out. Second, she must be smart by sitting at the front of the class. Third, I needed to pass chemistry so it was important for me to get to know her. I encouraged the guy sitting by her to trade seats and the next day, I was her new classroom neighbor. I felt the connection immediately. She, however, thought I was a goof and ignored me. Through persistence, I finally won her heart and eventually her hand in marriage. I also passed chemistry. As couples enter into marriage, a surge of emotional energy is experienced by three electrical currents: *Compassion, Communication and Conflict.*

THE CURRENT OF COMPASSION

To begin, the electrical current of compassion is measured by how deeply each spouse is willing to love the other. One dictionary defines love as, "To regard with warm affection."[116] In a Christian's life, the definition is much richer and more expressive. Romans 8:9 states "God commended His love for us in that while we were yet sinners, Christ died for us" (KJV). The Christian's true definition of love is not from Webster but from the perfect expression of love from the heavenly Father through Jesus Christ. While looking at those in love, an interesting observation is noticed. Over time, those dedicated in their love for each another will experience stronger and deeper love. From this principle, it appears that love, therefore, is not a spontaneous process but a caused reaction over time. Agape love is the outgrowth of a sound, wholesome thinking pattern about one's partner that is "based on a personal decision."[117] This kind of love requires effort and discipline. As Gary Chapman writes, "It involves an act of will and requires discipline, and it recognizes the need for personal growth . . . . Our most basic emotional need is not to fall in love but to be genuinely loved by another."[118] The lessons learned about spouses will depend greatly on the focus of one's attitude and study. "Marital problems easily arise if your thoughts and feelings are distorted; if your sub-titles reinforce a negative view of your partner and your marriage."[119] If one desires to find faults in his spouse, he will find them. If one desires to find the best in her spouse, she will find it. Critical attitudes are like faulty electrical connections and one runs the risk of a highly negatively charged marriage. Criticism involves "attacking someone's personality or character rather than a specific behavior, usually with blame."[120] According to Gottman, this is one way couples sabotage their marriages. Love, however, can be rekindled by concentrating on the strong qualities of each other because, as stated earlier, it is not a feeling but a decision. The Apostle Paul wrote in Philippians 4:6, "Summing it all up, friends, you'll do best by filling your minds and meditating on things true, noble, reputable, authentic, compelling, gracious, the best, not the worst; the beautiful, not the ugly; things to praise and not things to curse" (The Message). It is important to understand that loving each other but not learning from each other can keep the level of compassion very low. Eventually, the beginning emotional current of "being in love" can change into the "What did I ever see in you?" electrical surge that will shut down the operation of compassion in the relationship.

THE CURRENT OF COMMUNICATION

This leads us to the second current of communication. When two people date, there are rarely problems in communicating. But after marriage, somehow the "talking" ability seems to vanish. Why? Willard Harley, in his book *His Needs, Her Needs*, explains this shift. He writes, "During courtship women fall in love as a result of the time they spend exchanging conversation and affection . . . . When married, each partner has a right to expect the same loving care and attention . . . "[121]

Unfortunately, marriages show one or both spouses doing a complete flip-flop in actions and attitudes. It seems that spouses may start to take each other for granted which would explain the change from fantastic conversations during dating to the humdrum of marital talk. This humdrum communication problem takes two forms:

1. Lack of communication
2. Wrong type of communication (under pressure of anger, stress or shouting) H. Norman Wright explains,

> Communication is the link that creates a relationship between people. Communication helps us to become who and what we are and what we know. Every person who marries brings his or her own dictionary to the marriage. Unless the definitions are clarified, the words we speak to each other cannot be understood.[122]

Problems and conflicts in a marriage are not dangerous. The inability to communicate the conflicting issues will lead to the destruction of trust, intimacy, and homes. "When divorced couples were asked 'Why did your marriage fail?' 86 percent said it was due to deficient communication."[123] This electrical current is designed to teach the tools of effective communication. It will also explore the love languages of the spouse and children. As implied earlier, the lessons learned from one's spouse will be communicated both verbally and non-verbally. Each spouse needs to be an active listener to create healthy communication patterns. Gary Chapman teaches a powerful communication tool called the five love languages. When spouses understand their love language and then desire to learn their spouses' love language, the flow of communication within the relationship is greatly enhanced. As an example, if a husband only spoke English and his wife only spoke German, there would be a language barrier. He could tell her all day long that he loved her in English but she would understand the message. If he, however, learned to speak to her in German and tell her of his love, she would immediately be able to understand and connect with him. This is the main principle of the five love languages. A husband will express his love to his wife in his own language. This may or may not meet the communication needs of the spouse and conflict can begin. The husband, in order to meet the communication needs of his wife, must become a student of her language and speak it daily. The five love languages, as described by Gary Chapman are *quality time, physical touch, gifts, words of affirmation* and *acts of service*. Couples that learn each other's love languages will greatly enhance the 'love-talk' rather than the 'silent-walk.'

THE CURRENT OF CONFLICT

The last electrical current is that of conflict. Some may ask, "Why are we looking at conflict. Shouldn't conflict be avoided?" No! In pre-marriage counseling, many couples, when asked about possible (and probable) marriage challenges would often reply, "Oh Chaplain, we love each other. We will not have any problems." Conflict in marriage is not something to avoid but something to expect. John Gottman writes, "Many couples equate a low level of conflict with happiness and believe the claim, 'we never fight' is a sign of marital health. But I believe that we grow in our relationships by reconciling our differences."[124] Because each spouse is unique, there will be conflict. "There will be numerous conflicts throughout the life of the marriage, and this is not bad, it is normal." [125] It is how you respond and deal with conflict that is the real issue. This last current, along with the current of compassion and communication, allow the heart to beat in a steady rhythm of successful emotional adjustments. Once the emotional adjustments are understood, there is a necessary move from the heart to the head in the marriage mental adjustments.

Mental Adjustments

One night, I was trying to get my brother, Mike, to turn out the lights so I could get some sleep. Mike, being five years older and three times bigger, told me that it was a perspective of "mind over matter." He put his hand on my shoulder and said, "I mind and you don't matter." Oh, the joys of brotherhood! This story does express a valuable lesson when it comes to mental adjustments. If the connections are to be right in the marriage relationship, there needs to be two distinct sockets to hook into. Like a lamp, one needs to have the right place where the energy comes out in order to make the light shine. Two sockets discussed in this lesson are the sockets of *Loyalty* and *Livelihood*.

THE SOCKET OF LOYALTY

The first socket demonstrates the position of both extended family and personal friends in this new, expanded world of marriage. This socket can either facilitate a strong electrical force or a family feud. Sometimes the greatest conflict within a marriage, aside from our personalities, can be with the in-laws. Hollywood has zeroed in on in-law problems by poking fun at parental relations and the havoc it can wreak on a marriage relationship. The sitcom *Everybody Loves Raymond* is a perfect example. But it's no laughing matter when it's part of a couple's real story. It can create marital problems that one did not anticipate and negative patterns of relating with one's new parents that can last for years. In her book, *Toxic In-Laws*, Susan Forward writes, "In my more than twenty years of counseling both individuals and couples . . . one indisputable fact has emerged true and clear. When you have in-law problems, you have marriage problems."[126] This is important due to the way one can project feelings toward the in-laws. These feelings will directly impact the relationship one will have with the spouse. Bad attitudes and unrealistic expectations can increase stress any time couples spend time with the in-laws. "It's only human to want love, acceptance, and generosity from the parents of the person we marry, and to feel bitter disappointment and resentment when those things don't materialize the way you had imagined."[127]

In dealing effectively with in-laws, it all starts with first working conflicts through with your spouse. Remember, you're in this together. A *Family Education* article on in-laws, reminded couples that working with your spouse regarding the parent's relationships was the key rule. Never put your spouse in a situation where he or she has to choose between you and a relative. If you do so, you're putting your spouse in a nearly impossible bind. Instead, try to understand the bond your spouse has with his or her grandparents, parents, and siblings. If possible, try to support that relationship. Even if your spouse has parents from hell, they are his or her parents.[128]

This can also lead to an interesting transformation that takes place when couples go to the old homestead for a visit. Dina Poch writes, "When you observe your 'better half' in the context of his family, it's like stepping inside *The Matrix*. You begin to understand how the family system functions…A light blinks in your head and you say, 'Aha! That is where he gets it from.' "[129] For example, a husband that became helpful and appreciative at home may change before his spouse's very eyes. If the rule of that household, while growing up, was that the women did all the work, a family peer pressure invades his personality and he will conform to the unwritten rules and expectations that he grew up with. Married couples need to break some of those unwritten rules and expectations that will harm the family's integrity. "Just as the doctor cuts the umbilical cord from the baby to the mother, so you must cut the umbilical cord of dependency and allegiance to your parents. If you don't, you run the risk of undermining the interdependence you are to build as a husband and wife."[130] According to Lee Wilson in *Family Dynamics Institute*, "First, marrying our spouse means we turn our loyalties to him or her. That doesn't mean we are not loyal to our parents, but that we place priority on our husband or wife."[131] One obvious step to leaving our parents that shows we place priority on our husband or wife is changing homes. Our attention and effort turn toward our family's well being and happiness and a central home together. Wilson continues by writing, "becoming one flesh, in addition to referring to a husband and wife joining sexually, suggests we should stand united with our spouse regardless of outside opinions. We are so united with our spouse it's as if the two of us are one person."[132] Even if other people, such as in-laws, disapprove or offer their opinions, couples make up their own decisions and stand by them, together. Healthy boundaries "with parents can be helpful, producing growth and building the relationship."[133] Regarding friends, moving from a singles mindset to the married mindset can take some time. The word "friendship" conjures up thoughts of honesty, vulnerability, companionship, and mutual respect. It also implies a certain outlaying of time and energy. C.S. Lewis said of friendship, "It is when we are doing things together that friendship springs up — painting, sailing ships, praying, philosophizing, and fighting shoulder to shoulder. Friends look in the same direction."[134] The friends that spouses have can either help or hurt a new marriage. This may not always be a point of contention because if couples date for a long period of time, they may have the same friends. This can be especially true if a couple dates within a church or Sunday school environment. A growing challenge to new marriages can be the unhealthy friendships some couples retain or develop. Some spouses, even after marriage, choose to go out with their single friends without the other spouse. This is not inherently bad but if left unchecked, it can lead to disaster. Alyson Weasley writes,

These kinds of friendships are obviously easier. Unlike your spouse, the other party has the luxury of being transparent and real without all of the other encumbrances and responsibilities of your family's life. We have no problem calling deep emotional intimacy between a spouse and another of the opposite sex wrong, however, if we're investing emotional capital in a same-sex relationship at the peril of the marriage, then that this also dangerous. In marriage the final question is 'Am I investing more emotional energy into husband than I am in a friend or child?' this aids us in discovering where one is investing most of her emotional energy.[135]

During a marriage counseling session I conducted while stationed at Fort Campbell, a newly married husband shared that he often went out with his single friends to the bar. The single men were trying to pick up other women and he, the only married man, was placed in a position of compromise. He asked what he should do. My encouragement to him was to develop friendships with other married couples. He followed this advice and started to have a better marriage because he was doing more with his wife and their new friends than he was without his wife with his old friends. This is not to suggest that when couples get married, they turn their backs on their single friends. What is suggested is couples surround themselves with other married couples to help in the transition from the single mind to the married mentality. This does, however, take energy and time. Charlie Bloom writes, "Many of us make the mistake of neglecting our old friends when we are immersed in our new romance. Even our most loyal friend will lose patience with us if we become unavailable to them for a long time."[136] In life, a person may have four different types of friendship relationships. First, there will be people who are acquaintances or those known at a distance. Second will be peers and professional relationships. Third are the good neighbors. These are the type of people that one just loves to be around. The last are the few dear and close friends. One bumper sticker reads, "If a man dies with one true friend, he dies rich. If he dies with two, he is indeed a wealthy man." John Maxwell taught that the law of the inner circle of friends would either lift you up or tear you down.[137] This 'friendship principle' is imperative to understand and accept regarding the personal friends of each spouse. For a man, the next best friend he should have should be a male, not a female. The same goes for the female. There have been countless innocent friendships that have developed into something further. In *The Enticement of the Forbidden*, Judy Starr wrote about the need for accountability for women by other women. "When setting up accountability, choose one or two mature Christian women with whom you can bare your soul and learn from their wisdom. Confiding your struggles to a person of the opposite sex invites disaster."[138] More will be discussed in the OJMT section regarding necessary boundaries to protect one's marriage.

THE SOCKET OF LIVELIHOOD

The second socket deals with financial responsibility. When my wife and I married, we thought our two incomes would produce greater financial freedom. The opposite happened. It seemed that money disappeared faster when we married than when we were single. "Finances can be to a marriage what a match is to gasoline-explosive!"[139] There may be a tendency for newlywed couples to buy right now what took their parents twenty years to purchase. This socket of trust is short-circuited when one or both of the spouses are irresponsible, selfish, or allow money to become the heart of the marriage. In 1 Timothy 6:10, we are told that " . . . the love of money is a root of all kinds of evil". Another principle that couples need to comprehend is "the misuse of money is the destroyer of many a marriage." Christian couples work most of their lives at communicating with one another as to what it means to be faithful stewards of God's resources. Chapter four devotes a complete section on finances and aids couples in the foundation of financial responsibility.

PHYSICAL ADJUSTMENTs

In the world of wires and connectors, there are male adaptors and the female adaptors. These easily recognizable differences indicate a unique type of electrical connection. The differences between men and women are there to enhance the sexual relationship, not compete with it. Sexual intimacy is one of the greatest gifts given from God to a man and woman in marriage. Gary Chapman writes, "Intimacy is not sameness. Becoming close does not mean we become identical, that we lose our individuality, that are lives are blended into some new whole and we lose our personhood."[140] It is important to understand that God, the creator, made two sexes, as explained in Genesis 5:1-2. God designed each gender for a specific reason and purpose. The word *man* as it is used in this passage refers to humankind, not male persons only. Human beings were created in the likeness of God.

BE BIBLICAL IN SEX

In his book, *Tender Love*, Bill Hybels explains,
The duality of sexuality and spirituality is theologically incorrect. In Greek and Gnostic thought, body and soul

66

were separate. But the Bible does not teach this. It insists that spirituality involves all of what it means to be human, even sex, that seemingly most carnal of acts. There are no apologies or blushes about the issue[141]

God declares sexual intimacy pure and holy, as found in Hebrews 13:4. God and sex are connected. Why? God created sex and marriage. For a man and woman, sex is designed as a connector of body, mind and spirit. As Hybels states, "It has a ring of the divine."[142] This is also true when the couple no longer considers themselves newlyweds. One can cheapen the intimate relationship with an attitude of "self pleasure." God intended sexual intimacy for bonding (Gen2:24), pleasure (Prov.5:8) and procreation (Gen 1:28). In marriage, couples need to see God's design for the sexual relationship as a precious expression of intimacy and vulnerability between two people in the confines of holy matrimony.

BE "SUPER" NATURAL IN SEX

The thought, "doing what comes natural" does not automatically guarantee physical harmony in the marriage relationship. Philippians 2:3-7 and Ephesians 4:30-32 express that this relationship is so intimate that it is easy to be overly sensitive and easily offended. There must be a spirit of selflessness that permeates the relationship. Much research has been done on the sexual relationship. The stages of sexual response by Masters and Johnson are perhaps the most well known. In Human Sexual Response (1966), they detailed four stages of sexual response. They are Excitement, Plateau, Orgasm, and Resolution. [143] The Masters and Johnson model provides a helpful picture of how the body responds to sexual cues, but godly intimacy is interested in making love and not just having sex. Christopher and Rachel McCluskey state, "God has much more in store for His children that just a physical rush."[144] Spouses should plug this physiological model into a more comprehensive one that incorporates all four of the adjustment areas of married life. The McCluskeys have developed a principle that "the love-making cycle is not linear but circular. It places sex within the context of a committed marital relationship and shows it flowing out of love and intimacy a couple shares on every other plane of their marriage."[145] Only when spouses change from a mentality of self-gratification to a model of spouse-satisfaction does sexual intimacy becomes a primary socket of energy and excitement.

SPIRITUAL ADJUSTMENT

The most dangerous place on a cable is not the end but the cable itself. If there is an area on a cable that the protective coating is off, the underlining wires are exposed to the elements. This can cause a short circuit due to rain or other foreign matter that disrupts the flow of the electrical circuit. It can also be dangerous to someone that is working on the cable who touches it with bare hands and feels the power. In this area of spiritual adjustments, there are two spiritual coatings applied to the cable of attitude. This important covering holds the cable together to house the various wires of emotional adjustments and adaptors of the physical adjustments to the terminal of mental adjustments.

THE COATING OF COMMITMENT

The coating of Christian commitment has three important factors. These factors are cultivating spiritual depth, church life and a family altar. The first factor of cultivating spiritual depth involves incorporating God into the family faith system by establishing a home founded on the principle in Matthew 6:33. In seeking God first, lives will fall into place, the Christian witness will be empowered, and spiritual gifts and talents will become evident. Author Dallas Willard writes, "Spirituality is simply the holistic quality of human life as it was meant to be, at the center of which is our relation to God."[146] This factor of spiritual depth focuses on building God's kingdom by seeking God's will together, searching the scriptures together, praying together, and considering wise counsel together. A second factor is the church life of the married couple. Sometimes, young couples drop out of church life right after marriage.

When a couple attends church haphazardly and without a definite purpose or goal, their church experience can become disappointing. It is important for a couple to find a church home that will encourage spiritual growth. In *Knowing God Intimately*, the writer states, "Praise is associated with exuberant joy and thanksgiving. It is our response to what God has done for us. Worship, on the other hand, is the expression of reverential awe in the presence of God's glory and holiness. It is our response to the recognition of who God is."[147] This praise and worship is energized within the fellowship of believers at the local church. The "Log in the Fire" is a good illustration of this flame of energy and life. Many logs in a fire cause the flames to burn brighter and stronger. One can remove a burning log from the fire but the log's flames will soon die out. Why? Because the single log does not have the heat from the other burning logs to keep the fires going. This growth in church life will also impact the parents' encouragement of spiritual development of the children. A Barna

Group study regarding the spiritual matters in the life of children concluded the parents held themselves responsible for the teaching of beliefs.

The Barna study found that close to nine out of ten parents of children under age 13 (85%) believe they have the primary responsibility for teaching their children about religious beliefs and spiritual matters. Just 11% said their church is primarily responsible, and 1% said it is mostly the domain of their child's school. Few parents assigned such responsibility to friends, society or the media. Nearly all parents of children under the age of 13 — 96% — contend that they have the primary responsibility for teaching their children values. Just 1% said their church has that task and 1% assigned that role to the child's school.[148] How important is the church experience in the life of the marriage? The first place to look may be in the experiences of the child. A question raised is where the parents received their religious information to pass onto their children. Another study conducted by the Barna Research Group found that roughly seven out of ten American adults (71%) had a period of time during their childhood when they regularly attended a Christian church. Apparently, old habits die hard: a majority of those who attended church as a youngster still attend regularly today (61%), while a large majority of those who were not church-goers as children are still absent from churches today (78%). [149]

The last factor is the development of a family altar. One ideal place for you to learn to pray as an individual and as a family is at home. The family altar is not a piece of furniture with candles and incense. It is, however, a special time and location to initiate intimate spiritual oneness between you, the creator of the universe, and your family. This is where vulnerable, truthful, and open communication can take place. Regarding a study conducted on prayer, the following was published by the Barna group.

More than four out of five adults (83%) pray during a typical week. (2007) Women (89%) are more likely than are men (77%) to pray in a given week. (2007) Blacks (94%) are more likely than whites (83%), Hispanics (81%) or Asians (58%) to pray in a given week. (2006) Residents of the South (91%) are the most likely to pray in a typical week compared to residents of the Midwest (84%), Northeast (80%), and West (71%) (2006) While 98% of born-again pray in a given week, 72% of non-born-again report that they have prayed in the past seven days. (2007)[150]

Philip Yancey writes in *Prayer: Does it Make A Difference*, "We pray because of such forces of evil, we have no more powerful way to bring together the two worlds, visible and invisible."[151] Prayer and devotions around the family altar is not so much a time to just read God's word to gain an intellectual understanding as it is for each member of the family to grow in a faith relationship with the heavenly Father. Clift Richards encourages families to move the devotion of scriptures from the realm of head-knowledge to heart-knowledge.[152] The following are three suggestions for making a family altar: establish time, location, and devotional resources; read a passage of scripture and/or discuss a spiritual truth or lesson together; learn how to pray together (both husband, wife, and family). "Through prayer, God gives us His peace, and that is one reason even self-sufficient people fall on their knees and pour out their hearts to Him."[153] With these three ingredients poured into the refining fire of grace, the covering of married life has its first layer of protection against the worldly elements of compromise.

THE COATING OF COMPASSION

A second layer of protection for the marriage cable of attitude is found in the primary ingredient of forgiveness. True compassion for others grows only from a heart that is willing to forgive others their trespasses. Forgiveness is the solidifying material used in this special coating of frayed cables and wires of hurt and pain. Terry Wardel states, "Forgiveness is directly related to our emotional well-being. Jesus taught that its importance cannot be over-emphasized or its practice over-done."[154] In Matthew 18:21-22, Jesus expressed to Peter that forgiveness should be extended regardless of the number of times one has been offended. This principle was also emphasized in John 21:15-17 when Jesus restored Peter. Forgiving and being forgiven cannot be separated. The life that is open to the love of God is open to loving others. Anything that we may need to forgive is only a shadow of the debt we have been forgiven. "Christians," Ken Sande claimed, "are the most forgiven people in the world. Therefore, we should be the most forgiving people in the world. As most of us know from experience, however, it is often difficult to forgive others genuinely and completely. We often find ourselves practicing a form of forgiveness that is neither biblical nor healing."[155] Sande continued with the explanation that forgiveness is not a feeling, it is not forgetting, and it is not excusing. It is, however, a decision that begins the walk of forgiveness that will take you through a life long process.[156]

THE GRADUATION

The graduation day from Basic Combat Training is one of honor and pride. The marching, the uniforms, the flags, and the spectators add to the thrill of the moment. Family and friends attend to cheer the graduating soldier and his accomplishments and encourage him in his next level of military training. Married couples do not have a special graduation service from their Basic Marriage Training phase but they do develop the confidence and competence for the next level of their training. What began as two individuals has now merged into the united team of husband and wife. There are still differences and adjustments to make but they have passed the BMT phase and now are ready to build on their experience and learning. As they leave the parade field, they walk toward the marriage bus that will take them to their next level of training, AMT.

CHAPTER THREE

ALMIGHTY'S MARRIAGE TRAINING

MILITARY ADVANCED INDIVIDUAL TRAINING

Soldiers arrive on the bus and discover the location for the next phase of their training. They have successfully completed their Basic Combat Training phase and now the next step of their military development is about to begin. During their orientation, they are introduced to the three important elements contained within this phase of training. First is preliminary training. This first element prepares the Soldiers for the future of their job. As an example, in the 91J Physical Therapy Military Occupational Skill (MOS), all soldiers cycle through a ten-week course called General Medical Orientation (GMO). During these ten weeks, men and women explore and examine the foundations of anatomy and physiology, simple biology, and the beginning process of medical procedures and care. This period of training is like an entrance exam. If they are unable to grasp the simple concepts of medical care, they will not be able to handle the complex procedures of physical therapy. This writer experienced the GMO training in 1987 with a group of 110 other soldiers. Only 83 graduated to the next level.

The second element in AIT is the textbook training. Here students attend lectures and lessons appropriate to the job skill. Again for the 91J skill set, the various medical manuals and standard operating procedures (SOP) provide the intellectual disciplines for the physical therapy classification. Each lesson and training stage is filled with pop quizzes and tests. The third and last element of AIT is technical training. During this part of the course, the various sections of medical procedures, modalities, and treatment plans are now put to the test. Treatment plans are created within the safe environment of the classroom and practiced on peers. This segment of training allows the physical therapy technician to practice new skills. It also provides the opportunity for him or her to play the patient and share the experience of future patients. If a person fails at this point of the training, he or she will not be recycled. The student will be transferred to another military occupation and re-trained for a different job. The reason for this is the potential for damage caused by failure to follow the crucial guidelines of the medical applications. Many treatments and procedures, if done incorrectly, can cause extreme harm or even death. This researcher began his 91J training with 72 soldiers and concluded with 50. Some failed out of the course during the textbook segment but many failed during the last element. The attrition rate was very high but the importance of safety for the patient was even higher. .

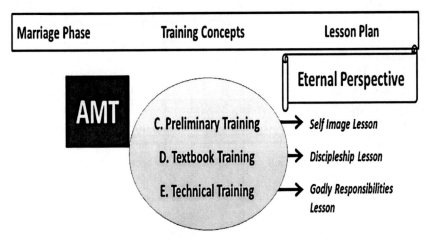

Figure 3.1 AMT

ALMIGHTY'S MARRIAGE TRAINING

Like the soldiers in the military AIT, couples enter into this new and diverse phase of marriage training. The Basic Marriage Training provided spouses with the rich understanding of how they and their mates are wired, the importance of building relationships, and adjusting to each other's differences. During the Almighty's Marriage Training (AMT) phase, God takes the husband and wife into a deeper relationship with Him to help the couple learn the life and death principles of marriage. As in the military version, the marriage AIT has three main elements: preliminary training in self-image, textbook training for discipleship, and technical training in responsibilities. The eternal themes of these three elements are worth, worship, and walk.

PRELIMINARY TRAINING: ETERNAL WORTH

While attending the General Medical Orientation portion of the military AIT phase, I was exposed to the big picture of medical military occupation. Here all soldiers gained an overall perspective of the medical world and its effect on life. As soldiers came into this element of training, they prepared for many skill sets within the hospital arena. Some would later walk toward the physical therapy position as this researcher did. Some would go on to study to become X-ray technicians; others would begin the journey toward becoming pharmacists. No matter the position, everyone needed to begin here at the base of the medical mountain, so to speak. It was from this vantage point that soldiers could look up and see the height, breadth, and width of the universal challenge before them. The primary step in this medical training sequence is the universal acceptance of the unique future skill one would learn.

Like the future military skill, every person has a unique need to be known, valued, accepted, and enjoyed by others. The development of self acceptance comes from what Phillip McGraw calls "defining moments."[157] He writes, "While it may be true that rewards and punishment teach us what to do, it is the defining moments that shape our internal behaviors. Defining moments anchor our emotional reactions to the world, either acceptance or rejection."[158] I believe that the need for acceptance is more than an emotional need. It is a spiritual need. Because of sin in our lives, our need for acceptance is desperate. Three things can hinder this acceptance. The first is fear. Fear of opening up and/or losing the other person's love and approval loom large but our most profound fear is that of being rejected. It is important to understand that the closer a person moves into a relationship, the more risk he or she will take. Fear is an attempt to keep the heart safe but it provides a false sense of security. Robert McGee suggests that everyone needs to develop the ability to look deep within the heart. "We may have the courage to examine ourselves and may desperately want to change but may be unsure of how or where to start. We may refuse to look honestly within for fear of what we'll find, or may be afraid that even if we can discover what's wrong, nothing can help us."[159]

The second major hindrance to acceptance is comparison. As men and women compare themselves with apparently successful people, perfect images from the TV, and unreal expectations, they create an unattainable standard.

These comparisons are what Dennis Rainey calls "personal phantoms."[160] These phantoms haunt a man or woman's life, keeping them hesitant and doubting themselves. Both fear and comparison are both exacerbated by the third hindrance—lack of understanding. The emotional and mental filters of one's own experiences and expectations often keep others from drawing close to us. One reason is because a person does not understand the true nature of man's heart. Another reason is the misunderstanding of God's grace or forgiveness. This affects how couples, families and friends model grace and forgiveness to each other. After a period of being rejected by others, a person may begin to feel that everyone rejects him and as a consequence, he rejects himself. The ultimate act of self-rejection is suicide. In the midst of this thick cloud of despair, the person has a hard time realizing that God accepts him so he develops a poor concept of God and finally rejects God. This can foster an attitude of bitterness, mistrust, and resentment toward God. In the first element of AMT, couples focus on three lessons that aid in developing a healthy self-image in relation to God, of self, and of their spouse.

SELF IMAGE AND GOD

The soldiers sit and look toward the front of the classroom. The instructor stands and, with a chart of the human body on the board, says, "Soldiers, this is the human body and here are the important areas of it. If you do not get this right, nothing will be right." This statement is especially true in a beginning marriage. If couples fail to grasp and understand the priceless value and eternal worth that God has given them, nothing in the world, including the marriage, will be right. We are receivers of God's love because that is how He created us. He also created us with the capacity to give love in return . . . . Our purpose on earth is not to dominate, but to receive God's love and to love Him in return."[161] Some men and women believe they are "too bad for God." Their comments that "God could never love a person like them" not only demonstrate a despairing view of life and love but also their rejection of God's truth regarding His love for them. McGee writes, "Since the Fall, man has often failed to turn to God for the truth about himself. Instead, he has looked to others to meet his inescapable need for self-worth."[162] If a husband or wife does not have the connection with God and the love He has for them in life, couples will short circuit the very energy source for a deeper love in the marriage. Some counselors argue this point since there seem to be many non-Christian marriages that are doing well without God. The first and greatest commandment in scripture is "Love the Lord your God will all your heart and with all your soul, and with all your strength" (Deut.6:5). It is in that aspect of loving God that we begin to understand the depth of love He has for us. Throughout the New Testament, we read, "But God demonstrates His own love toward us...." (Romans 5:8, NKJV), "For God so loved the world...." (John 3:16, KJV), and over a hundred other passages refer to God's love. A deep feeling of despair can come when a person accepts a false understanding of God's love. This not only destroys that person on the inside but also the outward relationships. God loves all people and accepts them as they are but He loves them too much to leave them that way.

SELF IMAGE AND YOU

"The answer to body image is a spiritual healing; it's getting in touch with the fact that you are fearfully and wonderfully made."[163] As the military students file into the classroom at Fort Sam Houston, they notice various charts and pictures of the body. The intimidating title of the lecture is displayed across the board, "Anatomy and Physiology." Some of the soldiers groan as they remember horror stories about this section. The instructor comes in with a smile and moves to the front of the class. He reminds these future medical personnel of the importance of knowing the structure of the body. He, however, takes an unusual approach, asking one of the students come to the front of the room. He starts, "There is much to know about the human body but I bet you know more than you think. Show me where your lungs are. Now show me where your stomach is. Now show me where your heart is located." The nervous student shows the locations and then is asked to sit down. The teacher continues, "Before we understand the bodies of others, it is imperative for us to know our own. It is here we learn that Anatomy and Physiology is not an impersonal principle—it is a personal practice. We need to know about our own bodies before we can help others heal theirs."

As a couple begins to understand the love of God and the love they are to have for God, their lives begin to change and their spiritual relationship becomes personal. It seems that Christians have a hard time talking about the love of self. "Many of use who are believers have an inferiority complex which we are constantly putting ourselves down, saying negative things about ourselves. This sense of inferiority is the product of centuries of teaching in the church that says that it is wrong for us to love ourselves."[164] Such teaching equates self-deprecation with humility when in reality, the two are not the same. Self-deprecation says, 'I am nothing. I am worthless, useless, and with nothing of value to give to anyone.' Many consider self-love to be a conceited or arrogant attitude fueled by pride. High self-esteem is not a noisy conceit but a high sense of self-respect and a feeling of self-worth. When you have it deep inside, you are glad you are you. Conceit is but whitewash to cover a low self-worth. With high self-esteem, you do not waste time and energy impressing others; you already have value. As John Mason states, "Don't just look for miracles. You are a miracle . . . . Do not be awestruck by other people and try to copy them. Nobody can be as efficiently and effectively you as you can."[165] The essence of self-esteem is compassion for yourself. "When you have compassion for yourself, you understand and accept yourself."[166]

Self-esteem in children can prepare a child for success or failure as a human being. "Children's self esteem can be influenced greatly when they feel their parents believe in them and have hope for their future."[167] These results are often evident in the outward relationship demonstrated by the mom and dad. "No matter who you are, your parents (or the people that raised you) remain the most important people in your life. That is because they exert the strongest influence on how you feel about yourself."[168] In Leviticus 19:18, the second great commandment is to "love your neighbor as yourself" (NKJV). Ephesians 5:28 also states that men are to "love their own wives as their own bodies." Simply expressed, you cannot give what you do not have. This principle is especially true in the marriage relationship. If a wife does not love herself, she may find it difficult to fully love her husband. If a husband has acquiesced to feelings of self-rejection, he may not have the ability to accept his wife's affection. Norman Wright explains, "If you are a rejected person, you enter into marriage starved for love and acceptance."[169] This lesson is concerned with the causes of a poor self-image and its effects on a marriage. In most marriages, one or both partners struggle with self-acceptance. The results are often guilt, frustration, inability to communicate, fear, and general dissatisfaction. It can also cause one spouse to "make more demands on his mate for love and acceptance."[170] However, it is important to realize that although low self-esteem does not usually begin in marriage, it is often revealed in a greater way in marriage. Low self-esteem usually begins before kindergarten and frequently in the home. Author James Dobson states, "In reality, low self-esteem among women may be traced to thousands of causes, most of them linked with early home life in one way or another. The adult who never felt loved or respected as a child will never fully forget the experience."[171] Everyone longs to be accepted by others. Gary Smalley adds, "This yearning is especially true in our relationship with our parents. Gaining or missing out on parental approval has a tremendous effect on us . . . ."[172] Marriage, in later life, becomes like a mirror; you reflect your spouse's weaknesses, and he or she reflects yours. This can be painful, even more so if you suffer from a poor self-image.

Dennis Rainey said, "One of the greatest human needs we have is the need for unconditional love and acceptance. Unfortunately, many of us find that the fear of rejection can be a controlling influence in our lives and marriages. To break free of that negative influence requires commitment to an ongoing process of acceptance."[173] This "negative influence" often leads to self-rejection. Simply defined, it is self-devaluation and self-hate. These feelings can persist even after a person accepts Christ. A person can have a misconception of God and believe that He is a disapproving Father, waiting to chastise everyone who makes a mistake. Rainey also stated that "people may try to protect themselves from rejection, especially in marriage, by avoidance, putting on masks, lack of communication, seeking approval through performance, and keeping others emotionally distant."[174] One must understand that the first step toward emotional healing is to realize that God understands where the feelings are coming from and is broken-hearted about it. He wants to free us from the negative feelings that cause us pain. Yet the cure does not come from something achievable or obtainable from outside sources. No, the cure must come from inside because the problem is so deep-rooted. Only when husbands and wives come to the realization that they must love God first and then love themselves are they better equipped to love their spouses.

SELF IMAGE AND YOUR SPOUSE

In his book, *What Wives Wish Their Husbands Knew,* James Dobson explained some important factors that men need to understand about wives. He stated:

Women generally suffer from a poor self-image, more than men. There are three major reasons for this. First, their responsibilities as a homemaker have become matters of ridicule and disrespect. Second is the emphasis on beauty in society.[175]

How do you measure a woman? How do you measure her worth, her true beauty, and her total being? Historically, it's obvious that the criteria have often been very specific and restrictive. And today's society highlights this narrow point of view by many means. Simply stated, it is physical appearance. Movies, magazines, television, all bear constant witness to this external obsession. God's perspective on women, however, is far more comprehensive. "Obviously, God is not opposed to beauty, not even sensual beauty...Though part of what God saw was physical beauty (and the man and his wife were both naked and were not ashamed, Gen. 2:25, NASB) the most significant qualities were internal. This is obvious from the rest of the scripture."[176]

Dobson notes that the basic intelligence of women is also attacked.[177] He states there are primarily two negative ways to deal with low self-esteem. The first is withdrawal because of the perception of too many risks, such as the fear of failure or rejection. The second is fighting. This reaction fuels anger and later becomes a way of life.[178] In his book, *Bonding*, Donald Joy writes, "we tend to sabotage our best dreams for marriage . . . . We fall in love. We marry. But the wedding day tends to be the peak moment in marital satisfaction, so quickly the default replaces the deep hunger rooted in God's design of a man and woman."[179] People with low self-esteem are apt to feel responsible for their partner's unhappiness and to unwittingly sabotage their relationship as a result. Overly sensitive and insecure partners may read nonexistent meaning into their mates' ambiguous cues, thus leading their relationships to the outcomes they wish to avoid. While misreading cues may seem to be a greater danger in nascent relationships, researchers have found that even after ten years of marriage, "people with low self-esteem believe their partners love them far less than they actually do."[180]

So, when one spouse sees the other suffering from a poor self-image, what are some of the steps that spouse can be take to help the other? Dennis Rainey describes five effects that loving acceptance has on marriage:

I. Acceptance says I see you as you are and I receive you as God's gift to me.

> In Gen. 2:18: "And the Lord God said, 'It is not good that man should be alone; I will make him a helper comparable to him'" (NKJV). Couples need to believe that God is sovereign in bringing them together. Paul said, "Forgetting those things which are behind and reaching forward to those things which are ahead, I press toward the goal . . ." (Phil. 3:13-14, NKJV).

II. Acceptance says I see you as you are and I believe in you.

> I Cor. 13:7 states that love "believes all things." Believing in one another means being loyal, choosing to make the most of the best, praising the good and expecting great things because of who God is.

III. Acceptance says I see you as you are and I will try to understand you.

> Spouses' differences from each other complete the picture of the marital relationship. These differences can become a source of conflict if one spouse tries to make the other a carbon copy of him or her self.

I
V. Acceptance says I see you as you are and I forgive you.

> Couples are confronted with the question, "What do you think it means to forgive each other as God in Christ also has forgiven

you?" Without forgiveness, bitterness takes root in a person's heart, and he or she becomes unable to resolve any conflict in marriage or in life.

V. Acceptance says I see you as you are and I value you.

Why is "value" important in marriage? Because it is the very fragrance of worth that permeates the relationship. This blessing of acceptance will enhance the love and adoration the spouses have for each other. If the blessing of value is withheld, it will lead to the building of walls of resentment and bitterness.[181]

Bible Textbook Training: Discipleship

After graduating from the preliminary military training element, soldiers now progress to the next level. The focus of this element is on the plethora of information found in the numerous manuals, books, and military regulations. The textbook training element of the medical AIT involves non-stop articles, research, and medical cases. During the 91J textbook portion, the students were inundated with at least four main movements within the thousands of pages of medical knowledge. First, the class learned about the numerous body systems. Soldiers explored the endocrine system, respiratory system, and others. The most important was the circulatory system. Simply put, when the heart stops pumping, everything shuts down and dies. The next area of study was diet and exercise. These lessons were directed toward the patients and their pathways of recovery. They were filled with commands to "lift that leg, curl those toes, breathe in, and quit whining!" The role of proper nutrition in keeping the body healthy and recovering was emphasized. The Master Physical Fitness Trainer yelled, "You can run all you want but if you eat junk, you will be junk!" The right balance of nutrition aids the body's defenses against sickness and bad health. The third movement was the acceptance and application of medical procedures and exams. Under the supervision of the medical instructor, students examined patients (usually peers) to detect or affirm a specific issue. The student then developed plans to help educate the patient and explain the course of treatment. Finally, the class studied modalities and treatment plans. After the healthcare worker assesses a problem, a treatment plan for recovery is vital.

Like the soldiers, couples entering into the Bible Textbook Training element experience four similar movements. These training movements are not designed to develop doctors but rather disciples of Christ. Thus, as the soldier studies the body system, the couples focus on the very life everyone receives from God in salvation. The second movement, comparable to the exercise and nutrition unit, teaches couples about abundant life in God. The third unit equates to medical procedures and exams and facilitates an inspection and understanding of God's will in a couple's life. Lastly, the Bible Textbook Training movement equivalent to the study of modalities and treatment plans generates a strategy of service in married life.

The Body System: The Life from God

The circulatory system is the most important system in the body. It not only carries blood and nutrition throughout the limbs but also the most important ingredient for life — oxygen. If the heart stops pumping, this invisible gift we call air will not circulate to the limbs and other areas of the body, including the brain. Everything will eventually begin to die due to the lack of oxygen. Discipleship is the spiritual circulatory system in marriage at the point of salvation. It is the spiritual blood flow that feeds the passion for God and the studying of His Word. Consider the following picture of discipleship in the marriage relationship in *figure 3.2.*

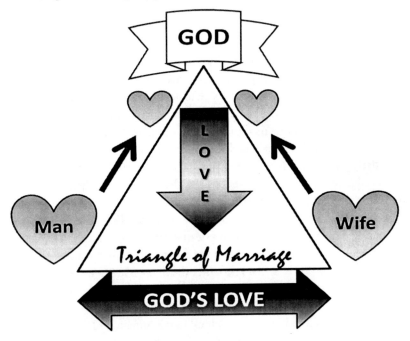

Figure 3.2. Discipleship in Marriage.

As a couple begins to draw closer to God in their individual relationships with Him, the man and wife will begin to draw closer to each other. Why is this true? Christians are not the same as other people in the world. This has been the scriptural position since the beginning of the New Testament church. Christian marriages are not like non-religious marriages. Paul writes in 1 Thessalonians 4:4-5, "Each of you should know how to possess his own vessel in sanctification and honor, not in passion of lust, like the gentiles who do not know God" (NKJV). Our marital relationships are holy and they are holy because our Christian commitments make them so. As author David Mains observes, "In a world that loudly shouts the opposite, Christian couples need to know that by following a Christian lifestyle and by developing their spiritual selves . . . they will reap untold benefits in their married lives."[182] Believers should not sit down just inside the gate of the garden of salvation. They should walk deeper and deeper into that garden to experience all the beauty of our relationship with God in Christ. After professing faith in Christ as Savior, everyone needs to go forward. Christians must exert strenuous effort to grow in every grace of the Christian life and never be satisfied until their lives display not just the mere talk of faith but also the fruits of faith in action. As Dietrich Bonhoeffer explained regarding a pastor, "If somebody asks him, 'where is your salvation, your righteousness?' he can never point to himself. He points to the Word of God in Jesus Christ, which assures him salvation and righteousness."[183] He continues to say that for the growing disciple, "The spiritual disciplines are those personal and corporate disciplines that promote spiritual growth. They are the habits of devotion and experiential Christianity that have been practiced by the people of God since biblical times. The Spiritual Disciplines are the God-given means we are to use for the Spirit-filled pursuit of Godliness."[184] The choice to accept Christ as Savior in one's heart and to live under His Lordship is a holy type of circulation system. Many have witnessed a bloodmobile drive into an area to collect blood donations. On the side of the bus it states that blood is the "gift of life." God, through His Son, Jesus Christ has given us the greatest gift— the gift of eternal life. One cannot earn salvation and God's love by consistent Christian living and spiritual growth but one can demonstrate the validity of that personal confession of faith. However, before a person can confirm that salvation, he or she needs to first encounter the living Christ and call on Him as Savior. Throughout the marriage, a couple that has developed a foundation of Christ in their lives will have the Holy Spirit guiding them throughout the tests, trials, and doubts. Circulation of the blood in the human body is an important part of growth. Exercise and diet, however, are important ways to keep the body healthy. It is also an important factor in the spiritual circulation of the soul.

EXERCISE AND NUTRITION: ABUNDANT LIFE IN GOD

Exercise is necessary for a healthy body but exercise alone will not do it. "More Americans are exercising now than ever . . . but we are still seeing a rapid increase in the number of Americans who are obese and who are suffering from health problems cause by being very unfit."[185] A healthy diet coupled with a consistent schedule for exercise helps create a healthy life. So why does it appear that few grasp this concept? Our society loves the Burger King™ motto, Have it Your Way™ , and they want it "My Way!" During the military medical instruction, the dietitian and physical therapist stated medical personnel need not only "to learn the principles of nutrition and exercise for patient education, but to learn it for life-long application." In his book, *Disciplines of a Godly Man*, R. Kent Hughes comments, "In today's world and church, disciplined Christian lives are the exception and not the rule."[186] As a couple accepts God's gift of life, they also exercise discipline in their lives so that they will grow spiritually. This growth plan is not a list of things to *do* but a focus of what to *become*. "Many people measure the fruitfulness of their lives by the quantity of their activities. This does not give a true picture. What you are is more important that what you do."[187] We will consider at least four areas of life discipline in this section: quiet time, prayer, obedience, and trials.

First, when couples are discussing quiet time, consider these three questions: *Why did God create me? Who should spend time alone with God? When and where should I/we have my/our quiet time?* Popular author Rick Warren puts it this way, "The purpose of a person's life is far greater than personal fulfillment, peace of mind, or even happiness. . . . If you want to know why you were placed on this planet, you must begin with God."[188] Scripture contains numerous examples of men and women spending time with God. In the New Testament, Jesus often went out early to spend time with the heavenly Father. Many Christian couples desire to grow in their walk with God and want to have a quiet time but often do not know how to begin. This is similar to the patient who looks at the doctor and says, "I want to get healthy but I do not know where to begin." Commencing a daily physical training (PT) program may start out exciting but the passion can wane quickly as the program becomes routine. Mental and physical conflict begins when the alarm clock goes off and the spirit says, "Go!" but the body shouts, "NO!" Spiritual training is as demanding in time and energy as physical PT, but is much more rewarding. As a young pastor, I realized that I needed to protect my minutes with God so I could last the hours with His children.

Second, couples need to develop a strong prayer life. "It is impossible to overstate the need for prayer in the fabric of family life."[189] It is not simply a shield against danger. A personal relationship with Jesus Christ is the cornerstone of marriage, giving meaning and purpose to every dimension of living. "Scripture insists that God has hardwired the universe in such a way that He works primarily through prayer. God has set up creation so that the way He does His work is through the prayers of His children. At the moment we pray, we become subject to the most powerful force in the universe."[190] Being able to bow in prayer as the day begins and/or ends gives us a chance to express frustrations and concerns that might otherwise not be vented. As James Dobson states, "On the other end of that prayer line is a loving Heavenly Father who has promised to hear and answer our petitions. In this day of disintegrating families on every side, we dare not try to make it on our own."[191]

Being inexperienced with quiet time, some husbands wonder how to pray. Matthew 6:5-13 provides a general background regarding the right and wrong ways to pray. God's Word directs us not to pray like the heathen or the hypocrite. For the heathen, the problem is vain repetition or thinking that God will hear because many words are used. The hypocrite's problem is praying to be seen by men instead of the Holy God. Their reward is the applause of men rather than the blessing of God:

> The hypocrite prays with the wrong motive; the heathen prays in the wrong manner. The hypocrite perverts the purpose of prayer. The heathen misunderstands the nature of prayer. The hypocrite prays to impress other people. The heathen prays to impress God.[192]

This type of prayer will lead to an imbalance in both an individual's and in a couple's life. Bill Hybels wrote, "Sensing the carelessness and one-sidedness of our prayers, we begin to feel guilty about praying. Guilt leads to faint-heartedness, and that, in turn, leads to prayerlessness."[193] True prayer is "built on the foundation of the sovereignty and character of God."[194] Prayer is a type of "spiritual breathing" that is unquestionably the most important activity we do every day.[195] The Apostle Paul encouraged us to "Pray without ceasing" (1 Thess. 5:17, NKJV). Paul did not say for Christians to "preach without ceasing" or "teach without ceasing" or even "have committee meetings without ceasing." Paul knew that there were incredible benefits to seeking and speaking with an awesome God.

So what benefits come from spouses praying together? The Bible is replete with instances in which Christians prayed together, usually to address common concerns such as healing, comfort, or release from prison. Scriptures like Matthew 26:36-46, Acts 16:22-30, and James 5:13-16 are some examples of people praying together. Another passage, John 15:1-4, reminds couples of the "vine and branch" perspective. As spouses pray together, they pass along spiritual nourishment to each other as they both draw from the same source of life. Praying couples will also experience a God that stops and listens to their words. Jesus himself assures us of that: "Ask, and it shall be given to you . . . " (Matthew 7:7, NKJV). Max Lucado wrote, "You may not turn the head of your teacher or keep the attention of your spouse. But when you pray, God pauses."[196]

Obedience is the third discipline, following right behind the actions of quiet time and prayer. Some couples may take this section of training lightly but there is a cost to disobedience. As in the human body, when the wrong items are ingested over time, the system will eventually be disrupted and perhaps even shut down. The effects of poor eating habits or life choices may not be experienced immediately, but eventually the toxins, stress, and strain will accomplish its work and the body will cease to function. Consider this promise from God's Word:

> Behold I set before you this day a blessing and a curse; a blessing if you obey the commandments of the Lord your God, which I command you this day, and a curse if ye will not obey the commandments of the Lord your God, but turn aside out of the way which I command you this day, to go after other gods, which ye have not know (Deuteronomy 11:26-28, NKJV).

St. Augustine's advice to "Love God, and do what you will" encapsulates a profound statement that a person who truly loves God will choose to obey Him.[197] The problems that separate us from God spring from our own disobedience. There is no middle ground when it comes to obedience. It is like the story in which the nurse asks a young woman if she is pregnant and the young woman replies, "I think so?" The nurse smiles and says, "Young lady, you either are or you are not. There is no middle ground here!" Obedience is doing exactly what God says to do immediately and with the right heart and attitude. Dietrich Bonhoeffer wrote, "Only he who believes is obedient, and only he who is obedient believes."[198]

Lastly, when a spouse studies God's Word in his quiet time, prays daily, and is obedient in all things, then he will experience trials in life. John Stott claims, "The astonishing idea current in some Christian circles today is that we can enjoy the benefits of Christ's salvation without accepting the challenge of His sovereign Lordship."[199] What is this challenge? It is to stand on faith in Christ when in time of trial or persecution. While I was a chaplain at Fort Campbell, KY, I was greatly amused by a young soldier I was counseling. The soldier explained all the trials in his life when he suddenly looked at me and said, "Chaplain, isn't it great that as God's man, you never have to face things like this!" Some misguided Christians believe the statement, "If you'll just give your life to Christ, all your problems will go away." Is that really true? No! However, some believers make the mistake of thinking that the Christian life will be a bed of roses without the thorns! Consider these words from Peter. "Dear Friends, don't be bewildered or surprised when you go through the fiery trials ahead, for this is no strange, unusual thing that is going to happen to you" (1 Peter 4:12, Living Bible). Turning and reversing the negative experiences of life into something positive actually gives new freedom and victory over damaging emotions like anger, worry, fear, and stress. This does not mean people will not have negative experiences or that they can escape pain. C.S. Lewis penned these words in his book, *A Grief Observed*, "Grief is like a long valley, a winding valley where any bend may reveal a totally new landscape."[200] This hopeful message tells readers that they can rid themselves of negativity and stop playing the blame game— they can begin to take those emotions and turn them into something good. A Christian's testimony of trust in God during times of stress, loss, and tragedy is just as needed in a hurting life as they are in times of blessing. It is during these tempest times the world watches Christians to see if they really believe what they say they believe. Faith in trials is the outward demonstration of the inward transformation.

MEDICAL PROCEDURES AND EXAMS: LIFE IN GOD'S WILL

As stated earlier, a medical practitioner must understand the importance of the SOAP note when assessing a patient. In the acronym SOAP, the S, standing for Subjective, is the main complaint that the patient brings to the doctor. This letter reminds the physician to gather some of the symptoms needed for future assessment. The O stands for Observation, which is what the medical professional is doing while the patient is either coming into the room or while talking with him or her. For example, if a physical therapist examined a soldier who stated after walking into the room, "I just can't walk. I have a terrible pain in my left ankle," the therapist would listen to the words of the patient while watching the patient's actions. The therapist would then move on to the letter A, conducting an Assessment of the patient. In this case, the therapist would take the patient through a series of tests, movements, and other fact-gathering procedures to obtain a clearer picture of the need. And if, for example, what the therapist saw was that the soldier entered the room limping on his right foot, not his left, and the assessment did not show any problem with either foot, the final determination would be that the soldier was faking and extra duty would be assigned for lying and malingering! In most cases, however, the therapist would find a real problem and move on to the P or Procedures that will be implemented to help the patient recover. This may include scheduling follow-up appointments, specific medication, or referral to another specialist.

In marriage, couples that desire to serve God in their lives often ask the question, "How can I know God's will for my life?" When a husband and wife take the time to conduct an internal ministry exam, God opens their eyes and places in front of them the will He has for their life. "Your love relationship with God prepares you to be involved in God's work by developing God-centered living. . . . You need to reach a point where you have no will of your own. Then God can cause you to desire His will above all else."[201] In his resource, *Basic Life Institutes in Youth Conflict*, Bill Gothard teaches various principles for knowing God's will in life. One principle states, "God is not obligated to reveal His will if you are unwilling to do it."[202] When a person goes to a doctor, the doctor may write a prescription for medication but the patient must fill the prescription and obey the directions in order to heal. God's will is not a spiritual cafeteria. Romans 12:1-2 provides a clear example of God's will. If a husband is not willing to do this, he will never know what God really wants for him. To know God's will demands total submission and obedience from each person. Anything else causes confusion, conflict, and frustration.

Another of Gothard's principles is, "God does not reveal His will for your whole life at one time."[203] The headlights on a car illustrate this point beautifully — they only shine for 100 feet and everything beyond that is dark. In Psalm 119:105, the psalmist states that God's Word is a "lamp unto my feet and a light unto my path" (NKJV). Light accepted brings more light but light rejected brings only darkness. Couples need to remember that God's will is primarily a relationship, not a position.

When a doctor concludes an examination, he or she usually provides a prescription for healing. The prescription for knowing God's will for couples in this portion of training is expressed in these 6 explanations:

1. God's will is always best. People reach their highest potential, are most successful and most happy if obedient to God's leading in their lives.

2. God is more willing for us to know His will than we are willing to know it. With God, there is no mystery or playing spiritual "Cat and Mouse." God simply wants the best for all.

3. God's will is usually revealed through normal means. Christian couples seeking God's will very rarely have a "Damascus Road" experience of a blinding light and a heavenly voice.

4. God's guidance usually comes one step at a time. You do not need to know about tomorrow as long as you walk in the light today.

5. God will always reveal His will in time for you to prepare for it. God always gives guidance but not always in advance. As Chuck Swindoll said, "We are all faced with a series of great opportunities brilliantly disguised as impossible situations."[204] Just remember that wherever God's will leads you.

6. God's grace will sustain you. Knowing God's will lies in our being willing to do His will. For couples, this is probably the most important lesson to learn both together and individually. Oswald Chambers said in his reflection on Romans 8:29, "All your circumstances are in the hand of God, therefore never think it strange the circumstances you are in."[205]

MODALITIES AND TREATMENT PLANS: THE LIFE FOR GOD

During the final days of the textbook training, the 91J students begin to discover the use of different modalities and equipment used for treatment. The ultrasound machine produces heat deep within the body that relaxes the muscles and stimulates blood flow to aid healing. Heating packs are placed on the patient's skin to make the underlying muscles pliable for stretching and exercise program, while ice packs are used after various therapy sessions to keep the swelling and pain to a minimum. The pelvic traction machine stretches the lower back and alleviates various back pains and impingements. Its use is also a wonderful and relaxing benefit after a hard day of patient coverage. In this section of learning, couples discover the numerous modalities of life, better known as spiritual gifts. In this portion of the training, couples begin to realize that they are to have a ministry in life, at home, and in the local church. They then go on to learn what particular ministry God has equipped them for, both individually and together.

When a medical specialist trains on each new piece of equipment, he or she has to concentrate on the instructions and the uses of the machine. For example, a machine for cervical traction would not be used on someone recovering from a total knee replacement. Nor should a patient who has a herniated disk in his lower back be put on an exercise bike. The right modality applied to the injury will lead to success rather than harm. In the service of God and His kingdom, couples are often frustrated because they want to serve God, but they find the areas of their service unsatisfying and aggravating. Often, it is not the place of service that is the problem, but that the person in that position does not have the spiritual gift for it. As in the medical examples above, sometimes the wrong modality is applied to the apparent need. Conversely, the right gift at the right time for the right reason will bring great satisfaction to the server and great impact to the body of believers. As Charles Swindoll explains, "Love brings the harmonious blending of diverse instruments into a symphonic unity. Without it, we sound like spoiled children harshly pounding the ivory keys of an exquisite piano. Instead of producing heartwarming music, we give people a headache."[206] God equips married Christian couples for ministry in at least four essential ways. First, God equips Christians with gifts for service. Romans 12 lists gifts such as prophecy, teaching, exhortation, financial means, and acts of mercy. These gifts are to be used for work and not kept secret or idolized. Each one represents something necessary if Christian ministry is to be complete and effective in people's lives. Second, God provides gifts for leadership. Ephesians 4 teaches about the spiritual gifts of apostles, prophets, evangelists, pastors, and teachers. Here the focus is on those people to whom God has given "special equipment" to help the rest carry on effective ministry: "the work of the ministry . . . the building up of the body of Christ . . . the unity of the faith . . . the knowledge of the Son of God . . . mature man/womanhood . . . the measure of the stature of the fullness of Christ" (Eph. 4:12-13, NKJV). The book of 1 Corinthians 12 examines a third group of gifts—those for power. These gifts include the utterance of wisdom, the utterance of knowledge, faith, healing, working of miracles, prophecy, and the ability to distinguish between spirits. According to Paul, God is equipping people for varieties of service. "We serve God by serving others, and we serve God by serving our spouse. God shapes us for service through a variety of methods, including our spiritual gifts, our passions, our abilities, our personality, and our experiences."[207] God's ministry is to do new things in an old world. 1 Peter 4 explains a fourth group of gifts—those for stewardship—that includes hospitality, speaking, and serving. Peter called people with these gifts "Stewards of God's varied Grace." God not only gave us grace in the forgiveness of sin but also in fitting us to serve Him.

As the Bible textbook element of the AIT phase draws to a close, couples begin to prepare for the next and most difficult element of the training phase. All of the teaching, briefing, and learning to date have been intellectual with some hands-on application. Understanding the body system helps set the stage for the heart and mind to work together for salvation. The exercise and nutrition segment provided the steps and resources for an abundant life in God. In the medical procedures and examinations piece, couples learned the importance of listening, watching, and assessing the will of God in the life of marriage. The final segment on modalities and treatment plans introduced the principle of the right spiritual gift for the right need in the service of God. All that remains is to assess what was taught, learned, and applied. The moment of truth has arrived; test time is here.

THE TECHNICAL TRAINING: GODLY RESPONSIBILITIES

The time finally comes and the head instructor for the Medical AIT School steps in front of his dedicated class and makes this announcement, "You have been undergoing many days of lessons and learning. It is now time to prove that we have not wasted our time teaching you. You are moving from the textbooks to the final element of this phase of training, the technical training. You will have two exams that encapsulate the entire time you have been here. The first exam will be on the lessons of the caregiver. This exam covers what you do as a medical caregiver and why you do it. This will be half of your final score. The second exam will be on the treatments. You will be tested in two areas. You will perform exams and treatments on your peers to demonstrate your competence in service. Then you will become the patient and demonstrate your confidence in the one performing the service. Simply put, you will heal your patient by becoming your patient. Now, let's get started!"

CAREGIVER LESSONS: THE GODLY ROLES OF HUSBAND AND WIFE

The couples file into a large room and on each table is the marriage exam. The tests are sealed and await the instructor's command to open and get started. Where there used to be talking, laughter, and jokes, there is now an eerie quiet. At the command "Begin," the exams are opened and the test of recall commences. The first question makes everyone sit back in his or her metal chairs and say, "Hmmmm." It begins,

A young wife, perplexed and visibly frustrated, asked, "How do I get my husband to be the spiritual head of the family? The question poses an interesting conundrum. How does the follower get the leader to lead? Women who ask this question often presuppose that their husbands are not interested in spiritual leadership.[208] While is it true that some men are not interested in this area of leadership, many Christian husbands are not only interested but concerned about fulfilling this responsibility. According to David Mains, Christian husbands can fall into one of the following 3 traps:

1. They do not have models that fit their contemporary marriage situation.

2. They don't have appropriate forums in which they can interact with and adapt ideas based on careful biblical study.

3. They have seen one form of leadership presented as the spiritual way and have found that this way does not match their unique, individual styles.[209]

Remember, when all else fails, go back to the primary instruction manual—the Bible. Society tries to pawn off many models as the right way for men and women to act. The problem with this philosophy is that it is based on a concept of self-satisfaction and not Savior-serving. "A good marriage is not one where perfection reigns; it is a relationship where a healthy perspective overlooks a multitude of unresolvables."[210] Some foundational passages for spiritual leadership are Ephesians 5:22-25, 1 Corinthians 11:3, Genesis 1:26-27, Galatians 3:24-28, and Colossians 3:18-22. Authors David and Karen Mains note,

The Apostle Paul revolutionized the known order and placed upon the shoulders of the male, as spiritual head, the primary responsibility for creating a marriage so harmonious, that it mirrors the relationship of Christ to His church. There are three and one-half verses of instruction for the women and eight and one-half verses for the men.[211]

PATIENT LESSONS: GODLY LIVING

After the first half of the testing is complete, the couples feel as though their brains have been squeezed and every bit of knowledge and energy has evaporated. But now it is time to prepare for the second half of the final exams. When the instructor comes into the room, he separates the class—men on one side and women on the other. Each person takes a number to determine who will be the patient and who will be the medical practitioner. The first part of the exam measures the competence shown in the medical procedures and the treatments. The second part evaluates the confidence the patient has for the practitioner. All the students know that they will need each other to pass this final exam. The same is also true in the marriage test of living. In order for both to pass, the husband and wife need to not only know their individual jobs and responsibilities, but they must also have an intimate understanding of the needs of their spouse. In this exam, it does not matter who is giving and who is receiving, the final grade applies to both partners. As the God-designated spiritual leader, the husband has been given the role of the medical practitioner who must assess the needs of his most special patient, his wife. He must ask himself, "Will I demonstrate competence in the position that God has given me? Will my wife display confidence in my abilities and my role as spiritual leader?" He is then handed a piece of paper upon which is written the needs of his "patient" (his wife) and the test begins.

Ephesians 5:33 states that husbands are to love their wives and wives are to respect their husbands. Seems easy enough, right? But this commonly cited verse makes a crucial point that is often overlooked: Men are to elevate their wives through Christ-like self-sacrifice so as to create an environment of shelter, nourishment, and mutuality that has her best interests at heart. Some men will use this passage as a heavy weight to hold a woman down. The passage, however, is designed to aid in lifting the wife. Its most elemental message urges both males and females to discover by means of loving self-sacrifice, a relationship so profound Paul declares it a mystery. Kent Hughes writes, "Marriage is a call to die, and a man who does not die for his wife does not come close to the love to which he is called. Christian vows are the inception of a lifelong practice of death, of giving over not only all you have, but all you are."[212] One mystery that couples face in marriage is learning how to uncover each other's needs. Men and women differ when it comes to their deepest relational needs. "If a husband's deepest need (respect) and a wife's deepest need (love) are fulfilled, their relationship is able to flourish. But when these needs are unmet, an unhealthy cycle begins. Chaos ensues and a cycle of marital decline begins."[213]

"When a woman feels unloved, she can react in ways that seem disrespectful to her husband. He then reacts to this assumed disrespect in ways that feel unloving to his wife."[214] The more she complains and criticizes, the more he shuts down and stonewalls. According to Carol Heffernan, the message the wife is trying to send is that she feels unloved at that moment, but she reacts in negative ways that equate to disrespect from a male perspective. "Sadly, all she is trying to convey is that she feels unloved and he isn't able to decode her message. So, how do you stop this common cycle once it has started? The answer is simple: Mutual understanding begins when wives respect their husbands and husbands love their wives."[215] One goal of this exam is to help couples better understand how to do that, thus putting an end to many disruptive cycles.

After the husband finishes, the couple switches roles and it is the wife's turn to don the medical robe and become the caregiver. She begins with a mind full of questions: "Will he respect me? Will he help me through this test? Can I trust him?"

It often starts with something small. Maybe she arrives home from a meeting to find that the kids aren't in bed yet. She thought her husband would have remembered the family's need to get up early and put the kids to bed on time. She is upset and communicates this to him. She thinks he's being irresponsible and making things harder for her in the morning. But he doesn't think it is such a big deal. He was playing with them and expected that they could nap sometime the following day. As the wife tries to explain her feelings, she sees that he is becoming upset with her for being upset with him! When she speaks, he rolls his eyes. He thinks she's nagging, and she thinks he's insensitive. And so it goes. Like many couples, they never saw it coming. These seemingly minor conflicts are like termites, silently eating away beneath the surface, until one day the foundation crumbles. The trouble is that this disagreement isn't only about the children's bedtime. It goes much deeper. The wife isn't just looking for a resolution on bedtime. At a certain point, she begins to feel unloved and thinks, "If I mattered to him, he'd be more attentive and would definitely talk to me." The husband, meanwhile, interprets his wife's "need to talk" as another situation that will result in him feeling disrespected as a person. He thinks, "I can never be good enough." According to Carol Hefferman, "A husband needs respect like he needs air to breathe, while love is by far a wife's greatest need. Without it, couples can easily get caught up in the constant back-and-forth of complaining and stonewalling, action and reaction."[216]

MAKING THE GRADE

As the military students exit the classroom at "Fort Sam", sighs of "I'm glad that's over!" echo through the hallway. Everyone gathers outside the testing room to await the final grades. Some Soldiers sit in groups and ask about certain questions. These are the ones that enjoyed the exam and hope to receive high marks. Still others discuss the tricky questions and worry about getting lower grades than they had hoped for. Some only want to pass, even if it is by one point. They have put in what they consider "just enough" study and preparation. They are also the ones that end up nervous at this point because they do not want to go into another job if they fail out of this medical training.

This also happens in the marriage test of lessons and living. Some couples come through the exams and seem to have a bounce to their steps. They enjoyed the learning and stretching and they desire to move onto the next level of training. Other couples become stuck in certain expectations and responsibilities and may feel cheated out of a good grade in marriage. A few just are trying to pass with the lowest possible score. They put into the test and their marriage only what is needed to pass, but then are surprised when their marriages fails.

During my experience at Fort Sam Houston, when the scores were posted, the smart crowd moved up to look first. They were confident that they did their best and they expect the best results. The others stepped forward slowly, trying to see their scores over the shoulders of those in front. They were relieved to have passed but they did not talk about their overall scores. The rest of the group does not find their names on the list at all. Instead, they were directed to "come into the office and see the instructor." These few moved in that direction and realized they had lost their positions and moved out of the program. They mentally kicked themselves for not trying hard enough, saying, "If I just had one more chance."

The crucial nature of the marriage exam cannot be overstated. If one or both spouses do not pay attention during the first cycle of training and fail the marriage exam, there may not be a re-take. A final grade of "F" will be given and the couple will experience the emotional and mental impact of a failed relationship. Tim Kimmel writes regarding the husband's fight for marriage, "It's a hand-to-hand, side-by-side commitment to our brides . . . . It is a daily battle to maintain the freshness of our love toward our wives when we have to do it in an arena that is so utterly hostile to the sanctity of marriage commitment."[217] Only those couples that have taken their training seriously and persevered with tenacity are prepared for the final stage of training —OJMT.

CHAPTER FOUR

ON-THE-JOB MARRIAGE TRAINING

ON-THE-JOB TRAINING

The graduating phase two soldiers prepare to leave the AIT training site. They have endured many grueling weeks and now are ready to embark on the last phase of their job training. The class that was gathered together in study halls and lesson groups is being dispersed. All students will receive new assignments that will place them somewhere in the United States. I was one of the two soldiers that received orders for Dwight David Eisenhower Army Medical Center at Fort Gordon, GA. As I left Fort Sam Houston and the other 48 members of the graduating class behind, I realized that the comfortable environment of the classroom would be replaced by the strange new world of the Army medical center.

After arriving on the reporting date and in-processing with the new company commander, my colleague and I made our way to the final set of instructors. During orientation, we meet three of the clinic's physical therapists and learned each had a specialty. As new students, we also meet the Chief of the section and sat down in her office for the command in-brief. After short introductions and the necessary military record review, the Chief got down to business.

"During the next three months," she began, "both of you will rotate through three sections — one section for each month. You will be graded at the completion of each rotation with either a 'Go' or 'No-Go.' The therapists who work here are the best in the area and they want both of you to succeed. But that success is up to you, not them. What you put into this training is what you will take away from this training. Do you both understand?" With a quick, "Yes Ma'am," we were dismissed to finish settling in.

Over the next few months, we experienced three rotations that furthered our medical training and the lessons learned in AIT. The first rotation allowed us to practice the principles of physical therapy. This training time provided us a better understanding of the overall picture of therapy for their various patients. As therapists-in-training, we put theory into practice which helped us to understand personal skills and limitations. The second rotation enabled us to perfect our therapy techniques. Here we worked with each patient in their treatment and rehab. I aided my patients in finding the inner strength needed to recover while also exposing the habits hurting the healing process. The third rotation stretched our administrative skills by requiring us to develop a clinic budget for ordering supplies and running the section. Each student in the 91J skill set has the potential for arriving at his or her permanent party location as the Non-Commissioned Officer in charge (NCOIC). Thus, it is important for each soldier to know how to run a clinic both administratively and medically. It was a lot for us as new technicians to take in, but we were up for the challenge.

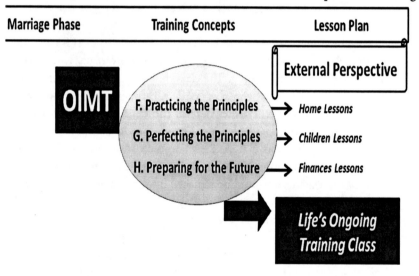

Firure 4.1. OJMP.

On-the-Job Marriage Training

Couples moving through the AMT phase of marriage training into this next phase are expected to take their relationship to a deeper level. The BMT and AMT phases of training helped spouses construct a solid foundation for their life. Now they will begin to build the structure of their home and family on this foundation.

As in the military OJT, the couples will experience three training rotations. The first will involve the practical application of the marriage principles learned in phases one and two. This rotation will provide the couple with hands-on-training to help them perceive and develop a clear picture of their marriage. The second rotation will allow the perfecting of techniques. No husband or wife becomes an expert on marriage simply by saying "I do." There is a learning curve and a lot of trial and error involved especially in the area of communication and children. During this rotation, couples will see the fruits of their marriage in the lives of their children. The fruit is not just the children themselves, but also the reflection of the parents' life views and practices as mirrored by the children. The third rotation will address the family's future financial preparation. Budgeting and forward financial planning allows a couple to build the life they envision without financially stressing the marriage.

Practicing the Marriage Principles: Building a Godly Home

Returning from their honeymoon, the newlyweds stop on the doorstep of their new house. Smiling, the husband scoops his wife into his arms and steps boldly across the threshold. As they enter, they hear the words of God, the Master Instructor, saying, "What you put into this marriage is what you will take away from this marriage. Do you both understand?" They shake their heads in unison and say, "I do!"

They find a roll of parchment paper on the dining room table. Sitting down, they unroll it to reveal the blueprints of their new house. Written across the top in bright red letters is a message from the builder: "I built the house but you both need to make it a *home*! If you want my help, follow the instructions provided." They realize that the note is attached to the blueprint contains a list. They read:

Step 1: Study the blueprints. Pay special attention to the four areas of structural integrity, foundation, commitment, communication, and building materials.

Step 2: Learn the principles for building, remodeling, and furnishing the home.

Step 3: Plant hedges. To do this, you must discover and enforce the property lines.

STEP 1:
STUDY THE BLUEPRINTS

The first step in making a house into a home is to examine the dynamics of structural integrity. The first area of structural integrity is the foundation. A building can be a beautiful piece of craftsmanship but if the foundation is not solid, it will fall apart during the first storm or tremor. One building company states, A house needs a foundation to shoulder its considerable weight, provide a flat and level base for construction, and separate wood-based materials from contact with the ground--contact that would otherwise cause rot and allow termite infestation. Depending upon when and where a house is built, the foundation may be made of stone, brick, preservative-treated lumber, concrete block, or poured concrete. If the foundation is not sturdy, the house can collapse over time.[218]

The security of a solid foundation, as spoken of in Matthew 7:24, cannot be overemphasized: "The rain came down, the streams rose, and the winds blew and beat against the house; yet it did not fall, because it had its foundation on the rock." Upon further examination of the blueprints, the couple notices the words "Christ-centered" written on the foundation. A scriptural reference follows: "Unless the Lord builds the house, its builders labor in vain" (Psalm 127:1). Both spouses then remember the AMT phase and the importance of spiritual growth in personal salvation and discipleship. They know that if they are to have a strong foundation (Christ) in this home, they will need to do more than remember the lessons of prayer, Bible study, and worship — they will need to put the lessons into practice. "With a Christ-centered relationship, other-centered attitude, and an unwavering commitment to making it work, your marriage can flourish — just as God designed."[219] Simply wanting to have a sturdy foundation will not build one. House plans can only become reality when the poles are set, the metal is laid, and the concrete is poured for the foundation.

The second area of structural integrity is commitment. These are the load-bearing pieces of the building that take the extra weight and disperse stresses of time and nature. Without these extra-fortified pieces of lumber, the house can easily weaken with each passing storm. Myler Munroe wrote, "We live in a disposable, cast-off-and-throw-away society that has largely lost any real sense of permanence."[220] For every ten new marriages in America, five will end in divorce. Does this mean that the other five will sail blissfully into the sunset? No. According to Neil Warren, all five stay together for a lifetime but will vary in degrees of disharmony. "Sadly, only two in ten couples will achieve what might be called 'intimacy' in their marriage."[221] Dobson writes:

> What will you do when unexpected tornadoes blow through your home, or when the doldrums leave your sails sagging and silent? Will you pack it in and go home to Mama? Will you pout and cry and seek ways to strike back? Or will your commitment hold you steady? These questions must be

addressed now, before Satan has an opportunity to put his noose of discouragement around your neck. Set your jaw and clench your fists. Nothing short of death must ever be permitted to come between the two of you.[222]

Communication is the third area of structural integrity. Everyone knows that important wires run everywhere throughout a house. In every room, in every corner, the wires ensure that the house is capable of using utilities such as gas, electric, telephone, and cable television. Sometimes a back-up generator system is installed to ensure that the house's electrical connections are maintained even when the power goes out. Houses are wired during construction while the walls are still only wooden studs. This makes it easy to see if there is a design or implementation problem and to make changes. Communication between spouses is not always quite so straightforward. Author John Gray reminds us that although spouses may use the same words, the way those words are used may produce misunderstandings. "Their expressions are similar but have different connotations or emotional emphasis."[223] Misinterpretation is a common communication problem, but if a couple strives to understand each other's wiring and that of their individual children (as learned in the BMT phase), glitches can be kept to a minimum. Short-circuits in the wiring will occur every once in a while, but the damage can be easily repaired if the marital foundation is strong.

The last area of structural integrity is building materials. The quality of the materials used will determine the quality of the product. Although all new houses look great, over a period of time those built with inferior materials will begin to deteriorate. If a builder cut corners by using cheap materials, expensive repairs will soon need to be made in order to stop the deterioration. So to, if couples try to use shortcuts when building memories, family experiences, or cultivating community, their time saved will ultimately be time lost. A cheapened attitude toward building will hurt both the home and the marriage. Myles explains, "the basic Greek word for 'marry' or 'marriage' is *gameo* which derives from the same root as the English word 'gem.'"[224] The home and the marriage must be created and crafted with the gems of love, faithfulness, fidelity, respect, and honor. Using these "priceless gems" as building material will ensure a quality structure.

STEP 2:
LEARN THE PRINCIPLES FOR BUILDING, REMODELING, AND FURNISHING THE HOME

An architect and a builder working together build a house. If they a reach using a different design for the house, the end result will be frustration and disaster. However, if they work in tandem on a unified design, the construction of the house will proceed quickly and efficiently. Thus, one of the essential steps of building is a good working relationship between the architect and the builder. Likewise in a marriage, the primary principle for building a home is oneness. Ecclesiastes 4:9-12 explains the power of unity in marriage. Solomon writes, "Two are better than one, because they have a good return for their work. If one falls down, his friend can help him up". Does this mean that there will never be disunity in a marriage? Absolutely not! What it does teach is that a godly home is not "created by finding a perfect, flawless person, but is created by allowing God's perfect love and acceptance to flow through one imperfect person, you, toward another imperfect person, your mate."[225]

In our modern, changing society, it is often necessary to remodel a home. During this time, couples need to review the status of each member in the household to see that everyone feels he or she is a VIP (Very Important Person) in the family. Family members can believe in themselves because this is where they belong, the 'in' group where they live, the people who like them, accept them, and trust them. When this is not true, some important remodeling must be done. It may be necessary to scrutinize family values, overhaul the emotional air conditioning system, renew the communication outlet, or sweep out old grudges. Couples must approach this remodeling with a godly desire to remove and replace any rotted wood and not simply patch the problem. No artificial front can stand the daily erosion of home life.

Every new home needs at least three furnishings. The first is a family altar of worship. In marriage, God seeks a couple's worship. During the BMT phase of spiritual adjustment, husbands and wives learn about the spiritual connections between each of them and God. This spiritual connection creates a place, a time, and a reason for a family time of worship that extends from the church into the home. A home also needs family traditions. Special family traditions that model biblical principles help family members, especially children, to feel a sense of belonging. Traditions bring a sense of purpose to a family's activities and helps couples pause in the midst of busy times. The third furnishing is the gym of family recreation. Most people have heard the phrase, "A family that prays together, stays together." Couples need to add another phrase: "A family that plays together will grow together." Family playtime is not only important for the kids, but it is necessary for the parents. During trips, events, and competitions, parents teach godly principles of winning, losing, and playing with integrity. They also demonstrate a quality lifestyle and make a lifetime of memories. When the remodeling is complete and the furnishings in place, couples can direct their attention to the outside of the home.

STEP 3:
PLANT HEDGES AND
ENFORCE THE PROPERTY LINES.

After the construction of a new home, there is a vast need for something green. The dust and dirt left after the construction can become an eyesore and a mud pit if left uncovered. Couples pay thousands of dollars for sod and foliage to be planted to transform the barren yard into a beautiful landscape. One type of foliage that is frequently planted is a hedge. Hedges not only add to the decor of the house but also provide something that all married couples need—privacy and protection. Somehow that simple green barrier helps families feel secure. Hedges also establish boundaries that run the length of the home's property line and establish the "out-of-bounds" region for the family. As with a house, husbands and wives must have well-established hedges of protection around the marital relationship. In his book, *Loving Your Marriage Enough to Protect It*, Jerry Jenkins states, "No one thinks he needs hedges until it is too late."[226] In today's society, sexual immorality hits frighteningly close to home. Without being aware of the need to protect them against it, couples are vulnerable. Just as it is "the little foxes that spoil the vine" (Song of Solomon 2:15, NKJV), so too seemingly small indiscretions add up to major traps.

Couples need to understand the definition and purpose of boundaries in marriage. First, what is a boundary? In the simplest sense, a boundary is a property line. It denotes the beginning and the end of something. If, for example, a husband goes down to the county courthouse and looks up his property, he can probably get a plot map showing the property lines. This delineates the dimensions of the property owned. In a marital relationship, if couples know where the relationship property lines are, they also know who has ownership of them. This ownership covers areas such as feelings, attitudes, and behavior. But boundaries in marriage are not about fixing, changing, or punishing your spouse. If you are not in control of yourself, the solution is not learning to control someone else. You can only control you. The most important boundary lines that we develop are the ones within our own personal life. These lines help couples to know what is and is not allowed in the relationship, which in turn, gives them the freedom to grow together in the marital relationship. To disregard these will lead to a Sampson-like experience. Sampson is a striking biblical example of a man who suffered disaster by forgetting the importance of personal boundaries. As one reads in Judges 13, his moral disintegration did not happen over night but was through a series of smaller boundary indiscretions. It is easy to blame Delilah for the fall of this mighty man but in truth, some twenty years before he saw Delilah, he made some boundary-breaking decisions. Let me explain. Sampson was special. In Judges 13:4-5, the angel of the Lord told the mother of Sampson,

> Indeed now you are barren and have borne no children, but you shall conceive and bear a son. Now therefore, please be careful not to drink wine or similar drink, and not to eat anything unclean. For behold, you shall conceive and bear a son, and no razor shall come upon his head, for the child shall be a Nazarite to God from the womb, and he shall begin to deliver Israel out of the hands of the Philistines (NASB).

A Nazarite was someone peculiarly set apart for the work of God. He was distinguished in holiness by the three vows he was to keep forever; Never to drink wine or even go near a vineyard, never to touch anything dead, never to cut his hair. These life vows (boundaries) were the outward representation of an inward commitment to holiness and righteousness. Sampson started to encroach on the boundaries in Judges 14:2 when he wanted his father to go and get a wife for him from the Philistines, the enemy. We then find Sampson walking through a vineyard in Judges 14 and later eating the honey from the dead lion carcass he killed from the vineyard experience (Judges 15). The fact is, when one says no to God in one area of his life, the boundaries start to weaken. One thing leads to another and one finds himself irretrievably on the downgrade of complete compromise. Sampson was exactly like many today. Carried along by the passions of the moment, he somehow forgot that actions always have consequences. Those consequences may not be immediate, but they are sure and certain nonetheless. Secure boundaries allow the marital relationship to grow uninhibited. One of the greatest and most needed protections provided by godly boundaries is from the destructive attitude of divorce. James Dobson writes,

> Don't permit the possibility of divorce to enter your thinking. Even in moments of great conflict and discouragement, divorce is no solution. It merely substitutes a new set of miseries for the ones left behind. Guard your relationship against erosion as though you were defending your very lives. Yes, you can make it together. Not only can you survive, but you can keep your love alive if you give it priority in your system of values.[227]

The Psalmist expressed, "... may your love and your truth always protect me" (Ps. 40:11). When protective boundaries are in place, the husband and wife and their children will not feel imprisoned but liberated to live.

Perfecting the Techniques: Raising Godly Children

MILITARY CLINICS AND PATIENTS

As the new physical therapy students, my partner and I began to work closely with the clinic's patients. We both learned the importance of having a prepared plan to help a patient in their rehabilitation during the sessions. Rules and routines must be kept with discipline and consistency. I also realized that there is no generic treatment plan that works for every patient. Each patient has different responses to the modalities, different motivation to heal, and different capacity to learn. Sometimes, therapists need to inflict some physical pain in order to help a patient push through a plateau of recovery. In the end, the victories of seeing a stroke patient walk on his own, a burned patient begin a new life, or a chronic pain patient become pain-free are what each therapist strives for.

CHILDREN AND PARENTS

When a husband hears, "Guess who is going to be a new daddy?" the world changes fast and forever. Suddenly the principles of loving each other in marriage take on a higher level of understanding and a deeper level of commitment. Just as there are no generic treatment plans, there are no generic approaches to child rearing. Every child is "fearfully and wonderfully made" (Ps 139:14) and comes with his or her own special needs. An article on the website ChristianityToday.com summed it up well: To balance your roles as spouses and parents, you need two things: advance preparation and on-the-job training. No matter what season of marriage you're in, children will affect how you relate as husband and wife. And while kids do complicate life, the shared tasks of being both partners and parents can become the most rewarding experience you'll have as a couple.[228]

During the first five or six years of a child's life, he reflects his home environment. Parents are the child's first teachers. They teach him to walk, to talk, to listen, and to understand the meanings of words. They help the child explore and understand the world, and they guide him as he assimilates and interprets the information he learns each day. In a real sense, parents are the child's models. He imitates adult speech and gestures, and mirrors the ideas and values of his parents. Children will also mirror a parent's walk of faith. Dobson states, "Without question, the most valuable contribution parents can make to a child is to instill in them a genuine faith in Jesus Christ."[229] The best way for this to happen is to have both parents faithfully involved in the life of the child. In a national survey on America's children and key indicators of well being, the following was noted regarding the importance of two parents for child rearing:

In 2004, 73 million children under age 18 lived in the United States, 900,000 more than in 2000. Children under age 18 represented 25 percent of the population in 2004, down from a peak of 36 percent at the end of the baby boom in 1964. The number of children is projected to increase to 80 million and represent 24 percent of the population in 2020.

Living with two parents who are married to each other is associated with more favorable outcomes for children. (Italics added) The proportion of children under age 18 living with two married parents fell from 77 percent in 1980, to 73 percent in 1990, to 69 percent in 2000, to 67 percent in 2005. Among children under age 18 in 2005, 23 percent lived with only their mothers, 5 percent lived with only their fathers, and 4 percent lived with neither of their parents.

Births to unmarried women constituted 36 percent of all births in 2004, reaching a record high of nearly 1.5 million births. Over half of births to women in their early twenties and nearly 30 percent of births to women ages 25–29 were to unmarried women. Non-marital births by teenagers accounted for about half of non-marital births in 1970, but dropped to one-quarter in 2004.[230]

Marriage plays an important role in shaping children's most basic understanding of themselves and their role in a future marriage. In his book, *How to Behave So Your Children Will Too*, Sal Sever expresses that children learn by copying. "A child's potential to observe and imitate is a remarkable quality . . . children learn values, attitudes, personal preference, and even some habits by modeling."[231] He continues to explain that since children copy the behavior of people around them, how a parent acts toward his or her spouse develops a template for the child to follow in the future.[232] Therefore, a biblical perspective on the roles of a man and woman demonstrated through the lives of the parents seem critical to a child's success. Jack Canfield, author of *Chicken Soup for the Soul,* writes, "I have come to believe that most parents truly want to be loving, kind, compassionate . . . . The problem is that most parents have never had a course in the specific methods and techniques of interaction, communication, and discipline that produce compassionate, caring, honest, and fair parenting." [233] Parents teach respect by first showing that they respect each other and the child. Parents should treat children with as much dignity and courtesy as they would any adult. They also need to respect a child's opinion, listen to his ideas and confidences, and answer his questions. If moms and dads encourage a child's interests and stimulate his or her imagination, that child will be a secure, happy person in his or her own unique way.

Dorothy Nolte, author of the poem, *Children Learn What They Live*, writes, "I believe that each child is unique and has a center of creativity and wisdom that is his or hers alone. It is the privilege of the parents to witness the unfolding of their child's inner self and allow its beauty to shine forth in the world." [234] Being the parents of a young child is the most important job in the world. It has to be done in a few short years. The business of educating a child must be done right the first time. Children are like wet cement. Once the handprints are placed and the cement hardens, there is no taking it back. The only way to remove the handprints is to break the concrete apart and start over. Although there may be times when cycles of negative thoughts and actions from early life experiences need to be broken, it is imperative for parents to start their child's emotional, mental, physical and spiritual growth process in the right direction. During this generational building rotation of training, parents learn to perfect three techniques: Bringing up children, boundaries with children, and blessing their children.

BRINGING UP CHILDREN

Proverbs 22:6 is a very well known yet often misinterpreted verse. The literal Hebrew says, "Train up a child in his way and when he is old he will not depart from it." That is usually understood as: "Train up a child with moral standards and he'll stray and play like sin. When he's had his fill of loose living, he'll start going to church again."

What this verse actually means is to raise a child according to his or her particular abilities. Derek Kidner, a Hebrew scholar from Cambridge University says, "What Proverbs 22:6 is talking about is sensitivity and uniqueness in raising a child." [235]

All parents can give their children at least three gifts in the formative years of development. The first is that the parent can understand the child's personality. As in the BMT for the husband and wife relationship, learning the temperament and personality styles of each child will allow parents to better communicate and connect with their son's or daughter's emotional, mental, physical, and spiritual needs. In their book *Temperament Tools*, Stella Chess and Alexander Thomas provide four reasons why parents need to discover the hidden child within the child. They write,

> 1. *Temperament is responsible for a great deal of behavior.* Some children are born with more sensitive bodies where some are seemingly indestructible. Some, like the parent, may be extremely active.

> 2. *Understanding your child's temperament makes your job as a parent a lot easier.* Imagine that your baby is a mysterious island and you need a map to find your way around. Knowing your child's temperament allows you to navigate through difficult times of child rearing and to administer appropriate discipline.

> 3. *Temperament helps parents avoid the blame game.* There are no "good" or "bad" kids in terms of temperament. Just as airplanes, cars, and bikes have their own advantages and disadvantages, temperaments do also.

> 4. *Parents who understand temperament learn to prevent behavioral problems.* When parents respond appropriately to what their kids need, they are able to head off many of the "crisis" moments in family life. There will still be some "strong-willed children" to deal with but the impact, when children are understood, is that they will grow and thrive in life.[236]

The second gift is to uncover the love language of each child. As discussed earlier in Chapter Two's emotional adjustments section, the five love languages are quality time, touch, gifts, acts of services, and words of affirmation. Gary Chapman explains,   "Every child has a primary language of love, a way in which he or she understands a parent's love best. . . . As we will see, your child and mine need to know they are loved to develop into responsible adults."[237] He also reminds parents that all children have a primary love language but every child needs all five love languages spoken in their life. "Your child can receive love in all of the languages. Still, most children have a primary love language, one that speaks to them more loudly than the others. When you want to effectively meet your child's need for love, it is crucial to discover their primary love language."[238] To communicate with your child on this level not only helps the child grow but also the family. "Families that communicate effectively tend to have fewer problems, are more likely to address problems successfully when they arise, and enjoy being with each other more."[239] When tension comes into the home, parents should check to see if the love language was spoken to the child. If not, the source of the problem may become suddenly clearer.

The third gift is time. In a world that seems to have less and less time, parents must protect the time they have with their children before they grow up and move out. Bruce Van Patter, in his article *Parents and Children*, explains how time can slip away.

> *1. Lack of leisure time.* Kids are kept busy. After-school programs, sports teams, and homework keep kids from trouble and boredom. But boredom is often the first step to inventing fun. "Down time" is the ground where ideas grow. Seuss developed his love for drawing by simply hanging out at a local zoo with his dad.

> *2. Readiness of electronic entertainment.* When kids do have unscheduled time, fun is just an on-button away. Television, video games, and computers (called "screens" in our house) give kids instant enjoyment. Such entertainment can be good, but it can only go so far. It locks kids into someone else's ideas and keeps them from exploring their own. As Joyce Myers expressed, "A #2 pencil and an imagination can take you anywhere."

> *3. A focus on product not process.* Schools are under tremendous pressure to get kids to test well. Many teachers I talk to wonder how a child will learn to think creatively if there is little time for "open-ended problems" — questions that have many possible answers. Parents, as well, often focus on final results. We cherish the finished painting over the pages of messy sketches. [240]

Unless parents spend time with their children, it is almost impossible to develop a deep relationship. "Spending time together is a decision that must be made and kept. We may have days when we prefer not to be with the family or feel we don't have time. In that case, we must evaluate how we spend our time and how we rearrange or eliminate areas in our schedule in order to be with the family."[241]

BOUNDARIES WITH CHILDREN

While parents grow in their understanding of the three gifts of personality traits, love languages, and time, it is important to simultaneously build boundaries around the heart and life of a child. The best way to safeguard the growth and development of children is through the boundaries of discipline. Stanley Coopersmith, associate professor of psychology at the University of California, studied 1738 normal middle-class boys and their families. He concluded that the ones with the highest self-esteem were those from disciplined families. He states, "Once the boundaries were established, there was freedom for the individual personalities to grow and develop."[242] David Miller wrote, "Good kids require good discipline. Tough kids require even better discipline."[243] Another author stated,

When properly applied, loving discipline works! It stimulates tender affection, made possible by mutual respect between a parent and a child. It bridges the gap which otherwise separates family members who should love and trust each other. It allows the God of our ancestors to be introduced to our children. It permits teachers to do the kind of job in the classroom for which they are commissioned. It encourages a child to respect other people and live as a responsible, constructive citizen.[244]

Author Bob Barnes writes, "Parenting is an overwhelming task and how to discipline our children is one of the most perplexing aspects of the job."[245] According to James Dobson, it's best to start disciplining your children when they're young, approximately 14 months of age. Youngsters are more pliable until they are around four years old. After that, the concrete hardens a little and you have to work harder at breaking it up. Discipline means teaching children that their actions have consequences. "What you do about a single indiscretion is not as important as what you teach on each occasion. Punishment may need to be a part of the discipline on certain occasions but it should follow promptly on the misbehavior. . . ."[246] If a parent withholds discipline from his or her child, the parent may regret the choice when the child becomes a teenager and decides that he or she just doesn't want to listen anymore. When there are no painful consequences to disobedience, children find it much easier to tune their parents out. Christian parents often think disciplining their children simply means not allowing the kids to do or to watch certain things. There is a place for prohibition but that is not the core of discipline; rather, it is to find a way to help the child experience negative consequences proportional to his bad behavior. Dobson explains that the goal of discipline "is not to control or break the will. The goal is to build within our children a wise, internal standard that will guide them when they have to make moral choices on their own."[247] For the task of discipline, parents would be wise to keep a large repertoire of strategies in their hats. What works for one child may not work for another

Developing a consistent approach to age-appropriate discipline is important. Author Karen Miller writes, "The fact is, disciplining a child can be challenging, and all of us have times we wish we were doing it better. I've learned, however, that the more we know about a child's age and developmental stage, the better we can tailor our discipline to fit him or her." [248] Miller goes on to say, "For consequences to mean something to your children, you need to know what your child can and can't understand. If you're feeling frustrated about an unwanted behavior, be sure that your expectations are age-appropriate."[249] Parents can read about child development, observe other kids, ask seasoned parents for advice, or find a mentor to help them figure out what their child is ready for.

LESSING THE CHILDREN

What does it mean to be blessed by your parents? What does it mean for a parent to bless their child? In biblical times, the practice of blessing was actually a parent's passing on leadership and property. This showed the child that the parent had great expectations for the child's future. Genesis 48 tells the story of Jacob blessing his two grandsons, the sons of Joseph.

One of the most touching pictures of blessing children is given in Mark's Gospel. When people were trying to bring their children to Jesus, some of the disciples scolded them. Jesus, however, reacted sharply and said, "Let the children come to me, and do not hinder them, for the Kingdom of God belongs to such as these" (Mark 10:14). Many kids are wounded because they sense that their parents don't even like them. Some examples are: a struggling student who watches his parents gloat about his sister's straight A's; a boy who strikes out in a softball game and sees his father's disappointment; an overweight daughter who repeatedly hears the command: "stop snacking so much if you even *care* about your looks." This absence of parental approval, or *family blessing*, can lead to untold pain.[250] Children who feel their parents' approval and love face the world with eagerness and confidence. Parents have the power to confer two essential blessings on their children: The blessings of love and of prayer.

The Blessing of Love

One of the best ways parents can show their children love and affirmation is to be accessible to them. Open arms, open hearts, and open ears provide the child a real display of love and are much more powerful than mere words. Smalley and Trent, in their book, *The Blessing*, share five important steps for parents to take to provide the blessing of love in a family.

Offer meaningful touch. The simple act of touching another person is key to communicating warmth and affirmation. It is even essential to physical health. Be generous with your hugs. "Every day researchers are discovering more and more information about the importance of touch. If we are serious about being a source of blessing to others, we must consider and put into practice these important points."[251]

Deliver good words. Hugs aren't enough. Tell your kids how you feel about them! "If you are a parent, your children desperately need to hear a spoken blessing from you."[252] Children who are left to fill in the blanks often feel worthless and insecure. At best, only confusion can come from silence.

Attach high value to your child. Tell your children about the qualities you admire in them. "Telling children they are valuable can be difficult for some parents."[253] One simple way to do this is to liken the child to a physical object. For example, you might call your daughter a "pearl *Picture a bright future for them.* Parents should explain why they think their child's gifts and character traits will be useful throughout the child's life. Avoid negative admonitions; inspire self-confidence.[254] *Make a commitment to stand by the child through the years.* This will help make the words of blessing become a reality. This will also teach the children that "God is personally concerned with their life and welfare."[255]

THE BLESSING OF PRAYER

Another important way for a parent to bless a child is by introducing prayer into family life. Fredrick Roberta writes, "Pray till prayer makes you forget your own wish and leave it or merge it in God's will."[256] A 1996 story in *Parenting* magazine reported that 65 percent of parents pray with their children before bed and at mealtimes. If a parent makes prayer a part of the child's lifestyle, talking to their heavenly Father becomes as naturally as eating or sleeping.[257] But children are not born knowing how to pray. Parents must first teach them. To do this, they must not only model prayers but the act of praying also. Children can memorize various prayers for mealtime and bedtime but they need a parent to teach them the power behind the prayer. Ephesians 3:20, 21 says, "Now to Him who is able to do exceedingly abundantly beyond all that we ask or think, according to the power that works within us, to Him be the glory in the church by Christ Jesus to all generations forever and ever, Amen" (NKJV). Dutch Sheets, author of the book, *Intercessory Prayer*, explains, "The word for 'exceedingly abundantly beyond' is the same word used for the abundant grace of God in Romans 5:20. The word is *hyperperissos. Perisso* means 'superabundant,' *huper* means 'beyond' or 'more than.' Together, they would mean superabundantly with more added to that."[258] This can only come about through the venue of a living example of a praying parent. Author Karen Linamen writes, "Created in the very image of God, we were created to pray.... We might even conclude that prayer is to the soul what breathing is to the body. In prayer, Christians exhale the worries, grief, and cares of their daily life then inhale the very presence of God."[259] When a parent is willing to call on God for His help and wisdom, it demonstrates dependency on the Lord and teaches the child to do the same. Although there may not be as many stressors in a young child's life, for a father or mother to demonstrate the right way to deal with fear, stress, or anger aids this future man or woman of God to do the same at their own point of need. It also encourages the child to develop his or her own special way of sharing and talking with God.

But it is not enough for a child to see the act of prayer modeled and to memorize the prayers of others. Children must also be given the chance to be themselves and pray in their own unique way. By offering a child this freedom, parents open a child's heart to a deeper and personal relationship with the heavenly Father. In her article, *Let the Children Pray*, Ester Ilnisky encourages parents to help their child learn to pray by following three simple guidelines. First, parents need to believe in the child's desire to pray. Children love to talk to God. Many kids have poured out their hearts in amazing, powerful ways when given the chance to pray on their own. Children will surprise parents with their excitement about prayer when given permission to speak what's in their hearts. Next, talk spiritual talk with your children. This demonstrates a recognition and respect of their spirituality. Saying things like, "You are a mighty young man/woman of God" or "You really have a gift for praying to God," lets a child know that God is alive in them right now. Asking questions like, "What is God saying to you or showing you from his Word?" or "How did you experience Jesus' presence and love today?" encourages them to look for God at work in their lives. Lastly, Ilnisky encourages parents to let children pray without prompting. They want to pray on their own, so resist the urge to guide their words. I am convinced that their refreshingly non-religious approach to God is their greatest gift.[260] Once parents have worked to lay a foundation for the home and a faith for the family, the last area of concentration is in the area of financial security for the future.

Preparing for the Future: Godly Finances

MILITARY ADMINISTRATION

Two military OJT students are called into the office of the clinic supervisor. He sits them down and hands them a piece of paper. On the page is a list of supplies, vending numbers, and a total of what the clinic has to spend. There is also a section that projects the various workloads, patient care plans, and modalities to be used. They scratch their heads and one finally asks, "What are all these numbers and items?" The clinical supervisor sits back in his chair with a smile as says, "Oh, those are the material needs for this next month here in the clinic. As future administrators of a physical therapy clinic, I need you to come up with a plan as to how I can meet the mission objectives for this month with the money that we have projected. Remember, there are many things to do but you will need to prioritize which ones to accomplish first to maximize the resources on hand." One of the students then asks, "Are you going to give us some time to work on this?" Again a slight smile creeps to the corners of the supervisor's mouth as he says, "Oh, yes. You have until tomorrow. I suggest you work together on it. You will brief me at 0800 here in the office. Have a great evening!"

MARRIAGE ADMINISTRATION

Money is one of the major causes of friction in a marriage, and it's no wonder. Living in a world in which we are constantly worried about taking care of ourselves, it is easy to forget that marriage is a commitment to forge a new life with another person. The lack of trust emanating from society has created prenuptial agreements and separate bank accounts. These undermine the commitment to a shared life with a spouse and are contrary to biblical teachings. Yet, the growing stress of bills, credit, and money is a never ending cycle in the American home. "Many people wind up reacting to events rather than designing and implementing a financial plan."[261] The key to understanding God's will in financial matters is the proper understanding of the word *stewardship*. As stated in Chapter One, a steward is "one who agrees to manage the property of another person."[262] The Christian couple is merely a steward of God's property while they live on earth. God can choose to entrust them with as little or as much as He desires, but in no case are we ever to take ownership. Christian financial expert Larry Burkett explains, "If Christians can accept that role of steward and manage God's resources according to His direction, God will continue to entrust us with even more . . . . Moreover, until the Christian acknowledges God's total ownership, he cannot experience God's direction in financial management."[263] As a couple prepares for the future, especially parenthood, they need to understand two things in order to establish a financial foundation—God's purpose in finances and God's principles in finances

GOD'S PURPOSE IN FINANCES

We are bombarded by advertising messages every day that attempt to entice us to indulge ourselves with whatever product is being sold. Advertisers play on the insecurities of consumers and tell us infinite ways their products will satisfy our needs and dissatisfactions. In response, we consumers spend with a vengeance. An article from *Focus on the Family* explained,

> Most impulsive spenders sabotage their own prosperity with the 'I want it now syndrome,' which is characterized by spending beyond their incomes. This, in turn, leads to persistent fear, unremitting debt and depression, and feeds into a downward cycle of worry and low self-esteem . . . the instant gratification of impulsive spending . . . deepening debt . . . more worry . . . more spending . . . .[264]

So often Christians get so involved in the day-to-day activities of earning a living and raising a family that they forget their real purpose in life—to serve God. They discover that their lives are out of balance and do not know how regain the balance. So, they buy more things or get rid of things in an attempt to find the balance. However, nothing seems to work. What will work is to follow the four primary purposes God has for His money in the lives of Christian couples:

PURPOSE 1: BASIC NEEDS.

Couples must learn to be content with what God has provided for them. "Husbands and wives need to establish a budget either together or with the approval of both. Every item should be discussed, prayed about, and agreed upon. The primary consideration should be to develop a fair, but reasonable, family spending plan and stick to it."[265] The aim of God's first purpose is to teach us about our attitude. "One of the great mysteries of Christianity is contentment. At least one must presume it is a mystery, because so few people live it. Yet contentment is not something that's found; it is an attitude."[266] Abundance or a lack of money does not affect our relationship to God, only our attitude does. "Christians get trapped into a discontented life by adopting worldly goals: more, bigger, and best. The Bible identifies these as indulgence, greed, and pride."[267] Immediately after accepting Christ as Savior, a person experiences peace and a real willingness and desire to commit everything to God. After a while, the person tends to fall back into the same old human routine of desiring and getting more, rationalizing that somehow he is still "serving the Lord." Evidence to the contrary consists of a lack of peace, a lack of spiritual growth, and a growing doubt about God's ability to provide. The Christian husband and wife must be able to trust God in every circumstance, believing that He loves them and gives only what they can spiritually handle. Larry Burkett states, "Because of its tangibility, money is a testing ground before God of our true willingness to surrender self to Him."[268]

PURPOSE 2: ILLUSTRATE GOD'S POWER.

God is not only the ultimate provider but He is also faithful to provide. Even when couples have been faithless in giving to Him, He has been ever faithful in His provisions. God uses money to help couples mature in their faith of Him and on Him.[269]
One of the great modern-day examples of this is the life of George Muller:

> One of the many fascinating aspects of George Müller's life is that it illustrates very simply the power of God. In 1834 George Müller founded the Scriptural Knowledge Society. However, the worsening cholera epidemic and the ever increasing number of homeless children caused him to realize immediate action was required and, in 1835, he called a public meeting with a view to opening an Orphan Home. This was a complete step in faith and, four days before the meeting, God confirmed that step through the Scripture—'Open wide your mouth and I will fill it' (Psalm 81 verse 10). By 1870 there were a total of five Houses at Ashley Down costing over £100,000 and housing more than 2,000 children. All the money and workers came as a direct result of prayer with no debts being incurred and no appeals or requests were ever made. There are many remarkable stories of the answers to prayer, and the buildings and the work continue to be a testimony to His faithfulness and the grace of God. George Müller received £1,500,000 in answer to prayer without ever needing to ask for funds.[270]

PURPOSE 3: UNITE CHRISTIANS.

"God has provided a ministry in money for many Christians, a ministry of giving. Once Christians accept giving as a ministry, a whole new area of God's

Word becomes clear."[271] Each local church has special needs. Couples are encouraged to watch the church and see what type of heart it has for giving. In the Old Testament, the Hebrew people brought approximately 23 percent of their increase to the Lord's storehouse, a physical storehouse. The keepers of the storehouse, the Levites, in turn used what was given to care for the widows, needy foreigners in the area, orphans, and themselves. In the New Testament, the people no longer brought their tithes and offerings to a physical storehouse; instead, they gave of their increase in tithes, offerings, and alms to the church body. The church then used the tithe for spreading the Gospel. The offerings were used for the general and administrative support of the church, and alms were used to care for the poor, widows, orphans, and the needy.[272] As a church reaches out and meets the needs of others, Paul's words to Timothy come alive, "Instruct them to do good, to be rich in good works, to be generous and ready to share" (1 Timothy 6:18, NASB).

PURPOSE 4: CONFIRM GOD'S DIRECTION

Normal life is filled with many distractions. Most, if not 99 percent, directly affect our families financially and change the direction we might take. Prayer is the best way for us to know what God would have us to do and the direction He would have us take. "Remember that God's perfect will may be best served by our need rather than our prosperity. To the Christian who is trusting Christ moment by moment, quality of life is totally independent of circumstances."[273] The ability to thank God in every circumstance demonstrates full dependence on Him, and the financial area is often used by God to develop maturity. God will provide for the need if it is in the direction He wants you to go. Ron Blue reminds couples that "money is not an end in itself. It's a tool which you can use to meet God's priorities."[274]

GOD'S PRINCIPLES IN FINANCES

God's Word provides standards for managing money that are essential for marital unity. If couples study these biblical principles, learn them, put them into practice, and adhere to those standards no matter how tempted they are to adopt the world's standards, their marriages will be strong and will remain sound. Ron Blue writes, "No amount of wealth will ever satisfy a person's basic needs for security and significance, which can only be met by God."[275] The following four principles are the minimum standards of finance found in God's Word.

PRINCIPLE 1:
GOD OWNS EVERYTHING.

"We have brought nothing into the world, so we cannot take anything out of it either" (1 Timothy 6:7, NKJV). Once couples accept the fact that God owns everything and that they have been chosen to be stewards or managers of God's property, it's important for them to manage according to His principles and standards. "There is a great amount of freedom when one knows and believes that God owns everything. It takes away the idea that 'I did it myself' or 'I am a self-made man.'"[276] Also, because a husband and wife become one in marriage, the financial assets and incomes of both husband and wife should be merged and they should operate from a unified financial base, rather than from separate and independent bases. God's Word describes the tithe as a testimony to God's ownership. In Genesis 14:20, Abraham acknowledged God's ownership through the vehicle of the tithe. Only then was God was able to direct and prosper Abraham and made him able to experience God's financial freedom. Couples must remember that God owns everything and they are only stewards; Also, tithing is giving back to God what is already His and that God supplies a surplus above basic needs in order that they may help others in need.[277]

PRINCIPLE 2:
THINK AHEAD AND AVOID PROBLEMS.

Scripture asks us, "Suppose one of you wants to build a tower. Will he not first sit down and estimate the cost to see if he has enough money to complete it" (Luke 14:28). Sometimes couples put off saving and planning until they are so deeply in debt that it looks impossible to get out. By then it seems too late to plan, except for crisis planning. "Spouses need to begin planning by writing down their goals and objectives, which should include a yearly balanced budget. This doesn't necessarily mean that they shouldn't borrow, but borrowing to buy consumables, such as gifts, vacations, and clothes, should be avoided."[278] This type of credit debt will put a couple into insurmountable debt faster than they can pay themselves out of it.

PRINCIPLE 3: KEEP GOOD RECORDS.

Again we read in the Old Testament, "By wisdom a house is built, and by understanding it is established; and by knowledge the rooms are filled with all precious and pleasant riches" (Proverbs 24:3-4).It is impossible for couples to have their finances under control unless they learn the basics of good bookkeeping. A recent survey discovered that less than two out of 10 couples actually know how to balance their checkbooks. This means that many married couples seldom know how much money they have to spend or how much they are spending. Couples should develop their financial plans together and work together, but there should be only one bookkeeper in the home who pays the bills. Two bookkeepers invite bookkeeping disaster.

PRINCIPLE 4: GET EDUCATED.

"The simple man believes anything, but a prudent man gives thought to his steps" (Proverbs 14:15). Most financially naive couples are not stupid regarding money; they are just ignorant and do not understand how borrowing and interest rates work. As a result, their primary concern becomes "How much are the monthly payments?" rather than "How much is this going to cost ultimately?" In addition, many times couples borrow more money than they can repay because they have no budget. "In essence, they have no idea where their money goes each month or how much credit their income can support. Couples need to learn financial management and budgeting skills and to use that information to avoid debt or financial problems."[279]

PHASE THREE GRADUATION

The day has finally arrived and the physical therapy students wait patiently for their names to be called to cross the stage. Many technicians and medical specialists are graduating this day and each waits with great anticipation to discover where they will serve next. With each military job skill identified, the graduates file across the platform to receive a diploma, a hand shake, and a set of orders sending them to their new duty station. Each graduate knows that this is the true beginning of their medical training. The past year has allowed them to learn a multitude of life lessons. In BCT, the soldiers discovered themselves and how to work with others. The AIT phase required them to open their minds and hearts to learn and receive the new skills and procedures for their future job. This last phase of OJT compiled all the materials taught and distilled it into personal and professional techniques that will be used to serve the medical community with pride. As each name is called, applause erupts, and the walk across a military stage begins.

Couples that reach the end of this intense year of marriage training feel the same way. Although they do not hold diplomas in their hands, their hearts are full of godly principles. The foundation of God's Word, aligned with the life of the married couple, starts a cycle in motion that should last a lifetime. The Christian husband and wife realize the impact of the three phases of training on their upward relationship with God, their internal relationship with self, and the outward relationship to the spouse and children. These three relationships create the triangular framework of a strong marriage that will serve as a continuous training cycle throughout their life together. Unlike the military graduation stage for the medical Soldiers, the stage for the graduating couple is life. As they walk across it, the love, life, and legacy that they leave behind in the lives of their children could be the final evidence as to how they learned, lived, and taught the eight principles of marriage.

CHAPTER FIVE
RESEARCH & FINDINGS
NATIONAL RESEARCH FINDINGS

In a time when it seems that more marriages are breaking apart rather than sealing together, the need for strong foundational marriages has never been higher. The rise, as indicated in the introduction, of divorce within the Christian community is staggering and the unraveling of the very tapestry of matrimony is taking place during the first six months of marriage. The growing statistics of divorce have reached an alarming number within the Christian churches. George Barna, president and founder of Barna Research Group, conducted the following research with a sample of 3614 adults. Barna's survey focused on the three-quarters of adults 18 years of age or older who have been married at least once. The study identified those who had been divorced; the age at which they were divorced; how many divorces they have experienced; and the age at which the born-again Christians had accepted Jesus Christ as their Savior. Comparing the ages when divorced adults had accepted Christ and when they underwent their divorce, the researchers were able to determine both the impact of one's faith commitment on the resilience of the marriage and whether the divorce occurred before or after their born-again commitment.

More Than One-Third Call It Quits

Among all adults 18 and older, three out of four (73%) have been married and half (51%) are currently married. (That does not include the 3% who are presently separated from their marriage partner.) Among those who have been married, more than one out of every three (35%) has also been divorced. One out of every five adults (18%) who has ever been divorced has been divorced multiple times. That represents 7% of all Americans who have been married. The average age at which people first dissolve their initial marriage tends to be in the early thirties. Among people in their mid-fifties or older, the median age of their first divorce was 34. Among Baby Boomers, millions more of whom are expected to get a divorce within the coming decade, the median age of the first divorce is currently 31. The Barna Group expects the average age of a first divorce among Boomers to be similar to that of the preceding generations by 2015, as the aging members of that generation sustain divorces later in life. The research revealed that Boomers continue to push the limits regarding the prevalence of divorce. Whereas just one-third (33%) of the married adults from the preceding two generations had experienced a divorce, almost half of all married Boomers (46%) have already undergone a marital split. This means Boomers are virtually certain to become the first generation for which a majority experienced a divorce. It appears that the generation following the Boomers will reach similar heights, since more than one-quarter of the married Baby Busters (27%) have already undergone a divorce, despite the fact that the youngest one-fifth of that generation has not even reached the average age of a first marriage.[280]

The various factors within society constantly attack the core of marriage with different perceptions of marriage, nuances of spousal roles and identities, and levels of commitment. The very fabric of the tapestry of marriage is in continuous strain to hold together under the growing pressure of new societal norms and changing values. The newlywed couples within a church are the future leaders and workers of the church and their early foundation in marriage is crucial for stability and security. Does this mean that if a couple completes this class, their marriage will not end in a divorce? The answer is no. However, the class will help the newly married couples to establish a better arsenal for the various attacks on them as persons, as a couple, and as a family. As many pastors will attest, the life-blood of a church is not the older generation. Although the wisdom and often the financial resources they provide are important, the church's lifeblood is found in reaching and teaching young couples. A variety of denominations have worked to reach out and teach to young couples the spiritual disciplines of their faith. Through Sunday school classes, Bible Studies, and workshops, many have been given the tools needed to build a strong faith. What is lacking in the local church is a program that enables newly married couples to focus their first year on the second most important decision (the first is their relationship with Christ) they have made in their lives to marry someone for life. The use of pre-marriage training has made a positive impact in the general world. Sharon Jayson, writer for *USA TODAY*, stated,

More couples are getting premarital education, perhaps thinking it may give their new marriages divorce protection. New research suggests they may well be right. Premarital education "is associated with higher levels of marital satisfaction, lower levels of destructive conflicts and higher levels of interpersonal commitment to spouses," says the study, published this spring in the *Journal of States*. Couples that received premarital education had a 31% lower chance of divorce. The number of hours spent in premarital programs ranged from as little as a few hours to 20 hours. The median was eight hours. Most religious denominations suggest that their engaged couples participate in such programs; Catholicism requires it. But now, others also are giving them a try. Unlike premarital counseling, which involves the couple alone and may focus on their conflicts and trouble spots, premarital education takes place in a group; classes provide general relationship advice. Because premarital education aims to lower the risk of divorce and identify problem areas before the wedding, experts suggest couples start such programs six months to a year out. [281]

A Military Perspective

The United States Army puts a high priority on training their troops to prepare for any contingency in the world. When notified, soldiers, equipment, and supplies have to be in the air within days of notification. The Army, as well as the other branches of service, has also come to understand the importance of marriage and family training. All the combat and skill training provided for the soldier will not aid him or her in combat if their focus is on a marriage that is dissolving back home. Soldiers that have a divided focus of mission essentials and marriage problems become a liability. Even the U.S. Army has discovered the importance of marriage education. The Army Chaplaincy developed a program to aid soldiers and their families adapt to the ever changing and intense culture of the military. The program, Building Strong and Ready Families (BSRF), concentrates on the highly charged areas of communication, conflict management, and children. In an article released in the *Armed Forces Press* in 2006, the marriage program is making a significant impact on military marriages.

WASHINGTON, Jan. 27, 2006 – Soldiers and their spouses are flocking to new and beefed-up programs to help them strengthen their marriages, and a dip in divorce rates appears to show it's having a positive effect, Army officials told American Forces Press Service. Divorce rates among Army officers dropped a whopping 61 percent last year following a 2004 spike that sent shudders through the service. In 2004,

3,325 Army officers divorced, but that number dropped to 1,292 in 2005, Army officials said. Divorces also were down slightly among enlisted members, from 7,152 in 2004 to 7,075 last year. Army spokesman Martha Rudd said percentages tell the story more clearly, particularly in the officer corps. In 2004, six percent of married officers divorced. In 2005, the figure dropped by more than half: 2.3 percent of married officers divorced.[282]

Newlywed Survey

The concepts for the "Power of the First Year" have been tested during the time frame of 1993 through 2002 at four locations, two civilian churches and two military post chapels. The two civilian churches were Williams Boulevard Baptist Church, Keener, LA (1993-5) and Bindlee Mountain Baptist Church, Morgan City, AL (1996-7). The two military posts were Memorial Chapel, Fort Campbell, KY (1998-99) and Ledward Barracks Community Chapel, Schweinfurt, Germany (2001-2002). Seven Christian couples participated in a research survey for the newlywed training: four civilian couples and three military couples. The couples were asked nine questions that ranged from the knowledge of the newlywed principles to the value of the training. The following pages contain the results of the survey.

The first question focused on the knowledge of each person prior to the beginning of the newlywed training. As indicated in the *figure 5.1*, the highest area of knowledge prior to the class was in the topic of discipleship in faith. From the range of 21% of "little knowledge" to 7% "very knowledgeable" indicated that each couple has a religious background prior to beginning the class. The principles that demonstrated the greatest need for education were: relationships of in-laws and extended families — 28%, and conflict management skills — 21%.   (See Figure 5.1 -- page 124)

The second question in *figure 5.2*, measured the increase of knowledge as a result of the newlywed training. The highest level of change was noted in the areas of conflict management techniques followed by responsibilities in marriage. Nine couples indicated a "large change" in knowledge in these two areas of concentration as indicated with percentages of 69% for the first and 64% for the second. (See Figure 5.2 -- page 124)

The third survey question asked, "Out of the eight foundational relationship principles, please rate them in the order of importance to your marriage." These left side headings displayed the training cycle of the newlywed training. The percentages to the right indicated the level of importance of each topic to the individual at the time of the training. For example, the normal flow of the training topics is: *Temperament, Marriage Adjustments, Self-Esteem, Discipleship, Godly Responsibilities, Home, Children* and *Finances*. As displayed in *figure 5.3*, the desired flow of the newlywed lessons indicated the top three topics (i.e. the one desired to be trained first, second, and third) were *Discipleship* (23%), *Temperament* (21%), and *Self-Esteem* (21%). The newlywed lessons that should be the last three trained (i.e. the 6-8 lessons) were *Home, Parenting,* and *Finances.* The sixth and seventh lesson dealing with home and children did not come as a surprise as most newlyweds did not have children during the first year of marriage. Although two of the seven couples did have small children, the majority of couples were without kids. (See Figure 5.3 -- page 124)

Figure 5.4 displays a series of three questions posed to the seven couples. The first question asked each individual to gauge the helpfulness of the eight training concepts in their marriage. Thirteen individuals indicated that the training was helpful in marriage. One individual indicated that it was not. It was interesting, however, that during the follow up question, "Would you recommend all newlyweds couples to attend a type of training such as this?" the total percentage was a 100% yes. This would indicate that the one individual that expressed that the class was not helpful may see the benefit for others to experience the training. The last question asked couples if they currently attend a church where this type of training is available. Two couples indicated 'yes' where the other five couples stated that they do not have this opportunity in their local church. (See Figure 5.4 -- page 125)

Question seven asked couples to share thoughts and provide additional comments for the newlywed training. This section of the survey allowed individuals to express in words what could not be indicated from the previous questions. Ten individuals out of fourteen responded to the question located in *figure 5.5*. (See Figure 5.5-- page 126)

The final question was essential for the conclusion of the survey results. The scope of marriage experience within the seven couples exceeded ten years of marriage as indicated in *figure 5.6.* The importance of this time ratio indicates that these couples have practiced the newlywed principles over a period of years. From the results found in question four, 92% have found them to be effective. The survey results were from Christian couples attending the newlywed class fourteen years ago. All of the couples surveyed now have children and are able to take the principles learned in the home and children section and build a legacy for their children's future marriages. (See Figure 5.6- page 126)

1. What was your knowledge level of the following marriage issues before attending the Newlywed Class?

	No Knowledge	Little Knowledge	Some Knowledge	Good Knowledge	Very Knowledgeable	Number of Respondents
Temperament/ Personality Styles	14% (2)	14% (2)	57% (8)	14% (2)	0% (0)	14
Marriage Adjustments	21% (3)	28% (4)	35% (5)	14% (2)	0% (0)	14
Godly Self-Esteem	14% (2)	28% (4)	42% (6)	14% (2)	0% (0)	14
Discipleship in Faith	0% (0)	21% (3)	28% (4)	42% (6)	7% (1)	14
Godly Marriage Responsibilities	7% (1)	14% (2)	50% (7)	28% (4)	0% (0)	14
Home Issues	7% (1)	35% (5)	35% (5)	21% (3)	0% (0)	14
Parenting Issues	14% (2)	42% (6)	28% (4)	14% (2)	0% (0)	14
In-Law/Extended Family Issues	28% (4)	35% (5)	28% (4)	7% (1)	0% (0)	14
Finances	21% (3)	21% (3)	35% (5)	21% (3)	0% (0)	14
Communication Techniques	15% (2)	53% (7)	23% (3)	7% (1)	0% (0)	13
Conflict Management Techniques	21% (3)	50% (7)	21% (3)	7% (1)	0% (0)	14

Number of Respondents	14
Number of Respondents who skipped this question	0

Figure 5.1

2. What was your knowledge of the following marriage issues after attending the Newlywed Class?

	No Change	Little Change	Some Change	Average Change	Large Change	Number o Respondent
Temperament/ Personality Styles	0% (0)	14% (2)	14% (2)	42% (6)	28% (4)	14
Marriage Adjustments	0% (0)	7% (1)	7% (1)	50% (7)	35% (5)	14
Godly Self-Esteem	0% (0)	7% (1)	23% (3)	53% (7)	15% (2)	13
Discipleship in Faith	0% (0)	7% (1)	21% (3)	42% (6)	28% (4)	14
Godly Marriage Responsibilities	0% (0)	7% (1)	7% (1)	21% (3)	64% (9)	14
Home Issues	0% (0)	7% (1)	14% (2)	57% (8)	21% (3)	14
Parenting Issues	0% (0)	14% (2)	14% (2)	28% (4)	42% (6)	14
In-Law/Extended Family Issues	0% (0)	21% (3)	7% (1)	57% (8)	14% (2)	14
Finances	0% (0)	0% (0)	21% (3)	57% (8)	21% (3)	14
Communication Techniques	0% (0)	0% (0)	14% (2)	35% (5)	50% (7)	14
Conflict Management Techniques	0% (0)	0% (0)	7% (1)	23% (3)	69% (9)	13

Number of Respondents	14
Number of Respondents who skipped this question	0

Figure 5.2

Out of the eight foundational relationship principles, please rate them in the order of importance to your marriage.	1	2	3	4	5	6	7	8	Number of Respondents
nperament/ rsonality Styles (why act the way we do)	7% (1)	21% (3)	7% (1)	0% (0)	7% (1)	21% (3)	21% (3)	14% (2)	14
arriage Adjustments mmunication and nflict techniques)	21% (3)	14% (2)	14% (2)	14% (2)	0% (0)	0% (0)	14% (2)	28% (4)	14
dly Self-Esteem w God's love pacts our love for ers)	0% (0)	0% (0)	21% (3)	35% (5)	0% (0)	14% (2)	7% (1)	21% (3)	14
cipleship (personal/ rital walk in faith)	23% (3)	7% (1)	15% (2)	0% (0)	23% (3)	0% (0)	0% (0)	30% (4)	13
dly Responsibilities hat God expects m the man and the man)	7% (1)	14% (2)	0% (0)	21% (3)	21% (3)	0% (0)	7% (1)	35% (5)	14
me (family/in-law ationships)	7% (1)	0% (0)	7% (1)	0% (0)	0% (0)	23% (3)	23% (3)	38% (5)	13
renting (how to raise odly child)	7% (1)	15% (2)	7% (1)	0% (0)	7% (1)	15% (2)	23% (3)	30% (4)	13
ances (how to thfully manage your ney)	7% (1)	0% (0)	7% (1)	0% (0)	14% (2)	21% (3)	0% (0)	50% (7)	14
								Number of Respondents	14

Figure 5.3

4. Do you feel that the Newlywed Class helped you in your marriage relationship?	% of Respondents	Number of Respondents
Yes	92.66%	13
No	7.14%	1
Number of respondents		14
Number of respondents who skipped this question		0

5. Would you recommend all newlywed couples to attend a type of training such as this?	% of Respondents	Number of Respondents
Yes	100.00%	14
No	0.00%	0
Number of respondents		14
Number of respondents who skipped this question		0

6. Do you currently attend a church that provides this type of training for newlywed couples?	% of Respondents	Number of Respondents
Yes	28.57%	4
No	71.43%	10
Number of respondents		14
Number of respondents who skipped this question		0

Figure 5.4

7. Please provide any comments regarding the newlywed class that you feel important to add to this survey study.

Number of respondents	10
Number of respondents who skipped this question	4

1. I learned more about my wife during the first months of the class than I did the whole year plus we were dating.

2. If you go through the class as newlyweds, I think you should do it again after children come into the picture.

3. I learned not to give up on my marriage too easily and that it takes a lot of work. But in the long run, it was well worth it!

4. One part of the class that I thought was great was the fact that it was taught by a married couple willing to be transparent about their own marriage. They modeled what they taught. They even let us see their weaknesses. This showed us that marriage and family are something you never stop working on and grown together in.

5. All churches should require pre-marital counseling by a licenses Christian counselor.

6. I know that we could have taken more away from it, but we both attended the whole thing. With my husband's job, he only attended some of the course and it was a very hard time for us, being apart so much. The insight was useful and we are grateful for all Godly direction when it comes to marriage.

7. To use this as a Sunday School class allowed my wife and I to grow together not only in our marriage, but also in our spiritual walk.

8. This was important in learning how to interact with your spouse.

9. This class does not have to be with just newlyweds. This is a great class for any couple to go through, even 5-6 years on marriage.

10. This study allowed my husband and I to learn about each other and also fellowship with other couples experiencing the same issues in marriage. It was very needed and helpful!

Figure 5.5

8. How long have you been married?	% of Respondents	Number of Respondents
1-3 years	0.00%	0
4-6 years	0.00%	0
7-9 years	0.00%	0
10-12 years	28.57%	4
13 or more years	71.43%	10
Number of respondents		14
Number of respondents who skipped this question		0

9. Do you have children?	% of Respondents	Number of Respondents
Yes	100.00%	14
No	0.00%	0
Number of respondents		14
Number of respondents who skipped this question		0

i Figure 5.6

CHAPTER SIX

CONCLUSION

MILITARY AND MARRIAGE

He was twenty when he entered into the military. Through his Basic Combat Training, he gathered the confidence and the discipline to push forward to his medical training in AIT and OJT. He was successful in both the academic environment in AIT and the hospital arena of OJT. At the end of the military training phases, he entered into a new type of training — marriage. As he and his new bride relocated to the Fox Army Hospital at Redstone Arsenal, Huntsville, AL, the excitement of both a new career and a new marriage was wonderful. During the first months, everything was good. There were many adjustments to the military schedule, the marriage, and the individual growth. As the young medical soldier began to become comfortable with his new position as NCOIC of the physical therapy clinic, he began to notice more and more conflicts in his marriage. The military had done an excellent job in preparing him for the challenges and conflicts of the hospital with various patients and procedures, but he was unprepared for the most important training ground in life — becoming a husband.

Although he came from a strong Christian family, he and his wife began to experience more and more tension within the relationship. As family issues arose, communication seemed to diminish and expectations were becoming disillusioned. The young couple joined Whitesburg Baptist Church and became part of a newlywed class. It was in this class that they learned more about each other in a few months than they had known in the previous two years of dating and engagement. The Sunday school teachers, Gordon and Jane Rose, began to work with this teachable and moldable couple to develop a variety of marriage principles and life-style practices. The couple grew, not only in their personal walk with the Lord, but also together in their covenant marriage relationship. The young Soldier and his wife became actively involved in the church, using their various gifts to teach, encourage, and train others throughout the three years that they were stationed in Alabama. Under the mentorship of the Roses, the young couple blossomed and began to work with other newlyweds and, later, the young man surrendered to the ministry call and became a pastor and, eventually, an Army Chaplain. Once retired, his calling was to help young couples grow in a growing church in the heart of the community he called home 26 years earlier.

PERSONAL REFLECTION

As one could guess from the beginning of this section, that young couple was my wife and I. Throughout these twenty eight years of marriage, the most important investments were the ones made during the first year of our relationship as husband and wife. There are and will be constant learning, re-fresher training, and challenging tests in future years but the covenant promise to "love, honor and cherish" remains strong and sure. Although more data can be produced, the need for marriage training during the first year is clearly self-evident. How is it, then, that the local church of Jesus Christ forgets this principle? In the smaller local churches, the need for workers is great and it is not uncommon for a newlywed couple to step into service of either teaching or leading a ministry right after marriage. This program established boundaries of service for the couple to ensure that they are focused on their marriage first. This investment of the first years is like planting the seed for a crop. It will take time but when the harvest comes, the fruit that it bears is more than one but may be "a hundred fold, some sixty, some thirty" (Matthew 13:23, KJV). The Apostle Paul expounds on the responsibilities of the husband and wife within the covenant relationship of marriage. The numerous chapters of Ephesians and 2 Corinthians have been quoted in weddings, sermons, and studies. If I am to look at marriage as Christ looks at the church, I need to dig deep within myself to discover who I am; what I am; what am I to do; and how do I do it. This is most important lesson when it comes to loving my wife as "Christ loved the church and gave himself for it" (Ephesians 5:25, KJV). To establish a newlywed class, two factors need to be considered. The first is the project location. The second is the cycle-style of the class.

NEWLYWED CLASS FACTORS

The first factor for establishing a newlywed class deals with location and setting. The location of the project can be in any church, any chapel, and any deployment at any time. Simply put, wherever the need exists, one can conduct this project. It thrives in a multitude of settings. As stated earlier, the use of this program can also be effective in either a local congregation or military chapel settings of any size. From any congregation, one can assess the need and then locate a few couples to begin this class. From experience, once the class begins, the growth of the class will come from the attendees and word of mouth. When a program is established with a set direction and ministry focus, the growth happens quickly. Regarding the civilian area, a good example was the newlywed class at Williams Boulevard Baptist Church, under the direction of Reverend Buford Easley. This class began with three couples and within two months, it had ten couples regularly attending the class. After six months, the class number was nineteen couples. Why did it grow so fast? The principle is easy. Where there is a need and the need is being met, people will flock to what is meeting the need. The primary audiences for this project are, but not limited to, newlyweds (married less than one year) and those engaged to be married (within three months). For the sake of this project, there is no limitation on the age of the couples. Although there will be some issues from those marrying later in life, the core established values of a strong marriage foundation will be the same regardless of whether the couples are in their twenties, thirties, or forties.

For use in the military arena, the garrison operations and chapel services can serve as a fruitful avenue for continuous marriage enrichment. Another productive location for this year-long class is during military deployments. The principles and lessons will enhance the couple's commitment to each other as one spouse encounters the class on deployment and then communicates the lessons and principles to the other spouse located at home. This will not only foster the level of commitment for each other but will deepen the communication to each other. This central purpose between the soldier and spouse will ultimately lead to a healthier and happier reunion after the mission is complete. Louis Ferrebee stated in his book *The Healthy Marriage* regarding success, "The answer begins with having a purpose, a shared marital mission that helps you to chart the course."[283] The intense stresses of deployments are difficult on a marriage. To add to that stress a break down of communication, aggravations, and hurt feelings can cause the spouses to suffer a broken home and marriage relationship. Ferrebee also writes "the real battle for a marriage to persevere is won or lost before a crisis occurs. A marriage that will crumble under intense pressure is similar to a China cup with a hairline fractures. While sitting on the table, the crack goes unnoticed. However, when the cup is help up to the light, the tiny cracks become visible. The light does not cause the cracks but illuminates a fracture that already exists."[284]

The second factor deals with the cycle-style of the class. The class is designed as a "cycle class." This means that a couple can enter the class at any point of the lessons and, when the lesson comes back around the following year, they will graduate to a new class. An example would be if a couple came into the class two months after it has begun, they would enter in during the "Self-Esteem" section. They would continue to go through the class until the section of "Self-Esteem" came around again. At that time, they would move to a new couples Bible study class or a place of service within the church. This cycle style has worked very well in the two church examples. There are some important boundaries placed within the life of the newlyweds regarding church service. Although this would not detract from a couple's service in areas of ministry of the church (i.e. Greeters, Evangelism, Choir, etc . . .) it would take the couple out of any teaching ministry for a year. This, again, was the case for a few of the couples at Williams Boulevard Baptist. One example was an engaged couple that had served in the Singles department as leaders. They made a commitment to focus on their marriage for the first year and then return to serving God with their gifts. This example caused some conflict with the Minister of Education and me. He was in need of teachers and did not like the idea of two of his best stopping for a year. This program will cause some changes within the ministry of the congregation. The most important change, however, is not in the actions of the congregation but in the attitude of the leadership. If the ministry staff is dedicated to the support and growth of young marriages, they will need to make every effort to provide the time for the newlyweds to learn and nurture their new relationship. Again, as stated earlier, if we allow the couple to invest the seed of marriage into the soil of their rich married lives, the harvest in the later years will be more than we realized. In short, the seeds of change allow the husband to begin with himself rather than try to change his spouse. Gary Chapman explains, "The most common reason people do not get the changes they desire is that they start at the wrong place."[285] David Hammons, one of the spouses from Williams Boulevard Baptist Church, had these words to say about the newlywed class experience. "It was one of the most helpful and practical Sunday school classes I've ever attended. It had the right balance between information offered and member input. I believe it really helped us get to know each other as a couple much better and faster. I'm so glad it was more than just lecture. I appreciated the activities and the assignments, which helped foster communication."

In conclusion, the power behind this class is not in the lessons or the focused principles. It lies within the very heart of the husband and wife that are attending these eight sessions. If each spouse is committed to learning and living the foundational truths of marriage, the year will produce a stronger marriage not for just the first year but for a lifetime.

BIBLIOGRAPHY

Anderson, Neil T. *Freedom From Fear*. Eugene, OR: Harvest House, 1999.

Augsburger, David. *Caring Enough to Forgive*. Ventura, CA: Regal Books, 1981.

Barnes, Robert. *Minute Meditations for Men*. Eugene, OR: Harvest House, 1998.

Blackaby, Henry T. and Claude V. King. *Experiencing God*. Nashville, TN: Broadman & Holman, 1994.

Bloom, Linda and Charlie Bloom. *101 Things I Wish I Knew Before I Got Married*. Novato, CA: New World Library, 2004.

Blue, Ron. *Mastering Your Money in Marriage*. Little Rock, AR: Family Ministry, 1990.

Bluestein, Jane. *The Parents Little Book of Lists: Do and Don'ts of Effective Parenting*. Deerfield Beach, FL: Health Communications, Inc., 1997.

Bonhoeffer, Dietrich. *Life Together*. San Francisco: HarperCollins, 1954.

_____. *The Cost of Discipleship*. New York: Simon and Schuster, 1995.

Bradshaw, John. *The Family*. Deerfield Beach, FL: Health Communications, 1998.

Brazelton, T. Berry. *Touchpoints*. New York: Addison-Wesley, 1992.

Burkett, Larry. *Investing in Your Future*. Wheaton, IL: Victory Books, 1992.

_____. *How to Manage Your Money*. Chicago: Moody Press, 1975.

Bush, Barbara. *Mastering Motherhood*. Grand Rapids, MI: Zondervan, 1981.

Chambers, Oswald, *My Utmost for His Highest*. Grand Rapids, MI: Discovery House, 1992.

Chapman, Gary. *Loving Solutions: Overcoming Barriers in Your Marriage*. Chicago: Northfield Publishing, 1998.

_____. *Now You Are Speaking My Language*. Nashville, TN: Broadman & Holman Publishing Group, 2007.

_____. *The Four Seasons of Marriage*. Wheaton, IL: Tyndale House, 2005.

Chapman, Gary and Ross Campbell. *The Five Love Languages of Children*. Chicago: Northfield Publishing, 1997.

Cloud, Henry and John Townsend. *Boundaries with Kids*. Grand Rapids, MI: Zondervan, 1998.

_____. *Boundaries in Marriage*. Grand Rapids, MI: Zondervan, 1999.

_____. *Boundaries in Marriage: Understanding the Choices*. Grand Rapids, MI: Zondervan, 1999.

_____. *How to Have that Difficult Conversation You've Been Avoiding*. Grand Rapids, MI: Zondervan, 2005.

Crabb, Larry and Dan B. Allender. *Hope When You're Hurting*. Grand Rapids, MI: Zondervan, 1996.

Crase, Dixie Ruth and Arthur H. Criscoe. *Parenting By Grace: Discipline and Spiritual Growth*. Nashville, TN: Lifeway Press, 1995.

Curter, William and Sandra Glahn. *Sexual Intimacy in Marriage*. Grand Rapids, MI: Kregel Publications, 1998.

Davis, Michele Weiner. *The Sex-Starved Marriage*. New York: Simon & Schuster, 2003.

Dettoni, John and Carol Dettoni. *Parenting Before and After Work*. Wheaton, IL: Victory Books, 1992.

Dillow, Linda. *Creative Counterpart*. Revised and Updated. Kansas City, MO: Thomas Nelson, 1986.

Dobson, James C. *Dare to Discipline*. Wheaton, IL: Tyndale House, 1971.

_____. *Love for a Lifetime*. Sisters, OR: Multnomah Press, 1998.

_____. *Love Must Be Tough: New Hope for Families in Crisis*. Waco, TX: Word Books, 1983.

_____. *Parenting the Strong-Willed Child*. New York: Contemporary Books, 2002.

_____. *Straight Talk: What Men Need to Know, What Women Should Understand*. Dallas: Word Publishing, 1991.

_____. *The New Hide and Seek*. Grand Rapids, MI: F. H. Revell, 2007.

_____. *What Wives Wish Their Husbands Knew About Women*. Wheaton, IL: Living Books, 1975.

Dobson, James and Shirley Dobson. *Night Light*. Sisters, OR: Multnomah Press, 2000.

Felder, Leonard. *When Difficult Relatives Happen to Good People*. Emmaus, PA: Rodale, 2003.

Foster, Cline and Jim Fay. *Parenting With Love and Logic*. Colorado Springs, CO: Pion Press, 2006.

Forward, Susan. *Toxic In-Laws*. New York: HarperCollins, 2002.

Gilbert, Larry. *Team Ministry: A Guide to Spiritual Gifts and Lay Involvement*. Lynchburg: Church Growth Institute, 1987.

Gillogy, Harold and Bette Gillogy. *Achieving God's Design for Marriage*. San Juan Capistrano, CA: Joy Publishing. 1995.

_____. *Experiencing Oneness: A Couples Guide for Growth in Intimacy*. Fountain Valley, CA: Joy Publishing, 1995.

Gray, John. *Men are From Mars and Women are From Venus*. New York: HarperCollins, 1992.

Gottman, John M. *The Seven Principles for Making Marriage Work*. New York: Three Rivers Press, 1999.

_____. *Why Marriages Succeed or Fail*. New York: Simon & Schuster, 1994.

Hughes, R. Kent. *Disciplines of a Godly Man*. Wheaton, IL: Crossway Books, 2001.

Hunt, Mary. *Debt-Proof Your Marriage*. Grand Rapids, MI: F. H. Revell, 2003.

Hunt, Susan. *Spiritual Mothering*. Wheaton, IL: Crossway Books, 1992.

Hunt, T.W. *The Doctrine of Prayer*. Nashville, TN: Convention Press, 1986.

Hybels, Bill. *Too Busy Not to Pray*. Leicester, UK: InterVarsity Press, 1994.

Hybels, Bill and Rob Wilkins. *God's Gift of Sexual Intimacy: Tender Love*. Chicago: Moody Press, 1993.

Jenkins, Jerry B. *Loving Your Marriage Enough to Protect It*. Chicago: Moody Press, 1993.

Joy, Donald M. *Bonding: Relationships in the Image of God*. Nappanee, IN: Evangel, 1999.

Keirsey, David. *Please Understand Me II: Temperament, Character, Intelligence*. Der Mar, CA: Prometheus Nemesis Book Co., 1998.

Kent, Carol. *Becoming a Woman of Influence.* Colorado Springs, CO: NavPress, 1990.

Kimmel, Tim. *Basic Training for a Few Good Men.* Nashville, TN: Thomas Nelson, 1997.

_____. *Grace-Based Parenting.* Nashville, TN: Thomas Nelson, 2004.

Kindig, Eileen Silvia. *Goodbye Prince Charming: The Journey Back From Disenchantment.* Colorado Springs, CO: Pinon Press, 1993.

LaHaye, Tim. *I Love You But Why Are We So Different.* Eugene, OR: Harvest House, 1991.

_____. *Spirit-Filled Temperament.* Wheaton, IL: Tyndale House, 1994.

_____. *Transformed Temperaments.* Wheaton, IL: Tyndale House, 1975.

_____. *Why You Act the Way You Do.* Wheaton, IL: Tyndale House, 1984.

LaHaye, Tim and Bob Phillips. *Anger is a Choice.* Grand Rapids, MI: Zondervan. 1982.

Lepine, Bob. *The Christian Husband: God's Vision for Loving and Caring for Your Wife.* Ann Arbor, MI: Servant Publications, 1999.

Lewis, C.S. *A Grief Observed.* London: Faber & Faber, 1961.

_____. *Mere Christianity.* New York: Macmillan, 1952.

Lewis, Gregg. *The Power of a Promise Kept.* Colorado Springs, CO: Focus on the Family, 1995.

Lewis, Gregg, Deborah Shaw Lewis, Jim Burns and Karen Dockrey. *How to Parent Your Teens Without Losing Your Mind.* Nashville, TN: Broadman & Holman, 2002.

Lewis, Robert. *Building Teamwork in Marriage.* Little Rock, AR: Family Ministry, 1989.

_____. *Raising a Modern-Day Knight*. Wheaton, IL: Tyndale House, 1997.

Linamen, Karen Scalf. *The Parent Warrior: Doing Spiritual Battle for Your Children*. Wheaton, IL: Victory Books, 1993.

Littauer, Florence. *Personality Plus*. Grand Rapids, MI: F.H. Revell. 1992.

Lucado, Max. *Turn*. Sisters, OR: Multnomah, 2005.

Markman, Howard J., Scott M. Stanley and Susan L. Blumberg. *Fighting for Your Marriage*. San Francisco: Jossey-Bass, 2001.

Mains, David and Karen Mains. *Building Your Mate's Self-Esteem*. Ventura, CA: Gospel Light, 1997.

_____. *Living, Loving, Leading*. Weston, Ontario, Canada: Cook Publishing, 1992.

Mason, John L. *You're Born an Original, Don't Die a Copy*. Altamonte Springs, FL: Insight International, 1993.

Maxwell, John C. *Partners in Prayer*. Nashville, TN: Thomas Nelson, 1996.

_____. *The 21 Indispensable Qualities of a Leader*. Nashville, TN: Nelson Business, 1999.

_____. *The 21 Irrefutable Laws of Leadership*. Nashville, TN: Thomas Nelson, 1998.

McCluskey, Christopher and Rachel McCluskey. *When Two Become One: Embracing Sexual Intimacy in Marriage*. Grand Rapids, MI: F. H. Revell, 2004.

McGee, Robert S. *The Search For Significance*. Nashville, TN: Thomas Nelson, 1998.

McGraw, Phillip. *Self Matters*. New York: Free Press, 2001.

McKay, Matthew and Patrick Fanning. *Self-Esteem*. 3rd ed. Oakland, CA: New Harbinger Publications, 2000.

Miller, David R. *Tough Kids.* Elgin, IL: Christian Parenting Books, 1993.

Miller, Sherod, Phyllis Miller, Elam W. Nunnally and Daniel B. Wackman. *Couple Communication I: Talking and Listening Together.* Evergreen, CO: Interpersonal Communication Programs, Inc., 1991.

Minsky, Marvin. *The Emotion Machine.* New York: Simon & Schuster, 2006.

Moore, Beth. *Living Beyond Yourself: Exploring the Fruit of the Spirit.* Nashville, TN: Lifeway Press, 1998.

Morley, Patrick. *The Man in the Mirror.* Grand Rapids, MI: Zondervan, 1997.

Munroe, Myles. *The Purpose and Power of Love and Marriage.* Shippensburg, PA: Destiny Image, 2002.

Myers, Isabel Briggs, Mary H. McCaulley, Naomi L. Quenk and Allen L. Hammer. *MBTI Manual: A Guide to the Development and Use of the Myers-Briggs Type Indicator.* 3rd ed. Palo Alto, CA: Consulting Psychologists Press, 1998.

Navigators. *The Character of a Christian: Design for Discipleship,* Book 4. Colorado Springs, CO: NavPress,1980.

Nee, Watchman. *The Spiritual Man,* vol. 2. Anaheim, CA: Living Stream Ministry, 1992.

Neville, Helen and Diane Clark Johnson. *Temperament Tools: Working with Your Child's Inborn Traits.* Seattle, WA: Parenting Press, 1998.

Nolte, Dorothy Law and Rachel Harris. *Children Learn What They Live.* New York: Workman Publishing, 1998.

Oerti, Ron. *Growing Strong in God's Family.* Colorado Springs, CO: NavPress, 1974.

Olson, David H. and Amy K. Olson. *Empowering Couples: Building on Your Strengths.* 2nd ed. Minneapolis, MN: Life Innovations, Inc., 2000.

Ortlund, Anne. *Disciplines of the Beautiful Woman.* Dallas: Word Publishing, 1984.

Parrott, Les and Leslie Parrott. *The Parent You Want to Be.* Grand Rapids, MI: Zondervan, 2007.

Peel, William Carr. *What God Does When Men Pray.* Colorado Springs, CO: NavPress, 1993.

Phillips, Bill. *Body for Life.* New York: HarperCollins, 1999.

Poch, Dina Koutas. *I Love My In-Laws.* New York: Owl Press, 2007.

Rainey, Dennis. *Homebuilders.* Little Rock, AR: FamilyLife, 1993.

_____. *Preparing for Marriage.* Little Rock, AR: Gospel Light, 1998.

Rainey, Dennis and Barbara Rainey. *Strengthening Your Mate's Self-Esteem.* Little Rock, AR: Family Ministry, 1989.

Ramsey, Dave. *Financial Peace Revisited.* New York: Viking, 2003.

Richards, Clift and Kathleen Richards. *Knowing God Intimately.* Tulsa, OK: Victory House, 2001.

Richardson, Ronald W. *Family Ties that Bind.* Vancouver, British Columbia, Canada: Self-Counsel Press, 1987.

Robie, Joan Hake. *What Would Jesus Do?* Lancaster, PA: Starburst Publishers, 1998.

Roseberg, Gary. Barbara Rosberg. *The 5 Love Needs of Men and Women.* Wheaton, IL: Tyndale House, 2000.

Sande, Ken. *The Peace Maker,* revised and updated. Grand Rapids, MI: Baker Books, 1991, 1997, 2004.

Schlessinger, Laura. *Bad Childhood, Good Life.* New York: HarperCollins, 2006.

Severe, Sal. *How to Behave So Your Children Will Too.* New York: Penguin Books, 2003.

Sheets, Dutch. *Intercessory Prayer.* Ventura, CA: Regal Books, 1997.

Smalley, Gary. *Change Your Heart, Change Your Life*. Nashville, TN: Thomas Nelson, 1997.

_____. *Homes of Honor*. Branson, MO: Smalley Relationship Center, 1996.

_____. *If He Only Knew: Understanding Your Wife*. Grand Rapids, MI: Zondervan, 1988.

_____. *Keys to Loving Relationships: Study Guide*. Branson, MO: Smalley Relationship Center, 1998.

_____. *Making Love Last Forever*. Nashville, TN: Lifeway Press, 1996.

_____. *Secrets to Lasting Love*. New York: Simon & Schuster, 2000.

_____. *The DNA of Relationships*. Wheaton, IL: Tyndale House, 2004.

Smalley, Gary and John Trent. *The Blessing*. Nashville, TN: Thomas Nelson, 1986.

_____. *The Hidden Value of a Man*. Wheaton, IL: Tyndale House, 1994.

_____. *The Language of Love*. Pomona, CA: Focus on the Family Publishing, 1988.

_____. *The Two Sides of Love*. Pomona, CA: Focus on the Family Publishing, 1990.

Smalley, Gary and Norma Smalley. *Decide to Love*. Grand Rapids, MI: Zondervan,1985.

Stanley, Charles. *The Wonderful Spirit-Filled Life*. Nashville, TN: Thomas Nelson Publishers, 1992.

Stoop, David. *What's He So Angry About?* Nashville, TN: Mooring Publishing, 1995.

Stott, John R.W. *Basic Christianity*. 2nd ed. Grand Rapids, MI: William B. Eerdmans, 1971.

Swindoll, Charles R. *Growing Deep in the Christian Life: Returning to Our Roots*. Portland, OR: Multnomah Press, 1986.

_____. *Improving Your Serve*. Dallas: Word Publishing, 1981.

_____. *Spiritual Gifts*. Waco, TX: Word Publishing, 1986.

_____. *Strike the Original Match*. Elgin, IL: David C. Cook, 1992.

Taylor, Jack R. *God's Miraculous Plan of Economy*. Nashville, TN: Broadman Press, 1975.

_____. *One Home Under God*. Nashville, TN: Broadman Press, 1974.

Thomas, Gary. *Sacred Marriage*. Grand Rapids, MI: Zondervan, 2000.

Tieger, Paul D. and Barbara Barron-Tieger. *Do What You Are: Discovering the Perfect Career for You Through the Secrets of Personality Type*. 3rd ed. New York: Little, Brown, 2001.

Walls, David. *Learning to Love: When Love Isn't Easy*. Wheaton, IL: Victor Books, 1992.

Wardle, Terry. *Wounded*. Camp Hill, PA: Christian Publication, 1994.

Warren, Rick. *The Purpose Driven Life*. Grand Rapids, MI: Zondervan, 2002.

Weber, Stu. *Four Pillars of a Man's Heart*. Sisters, OR: Multnomah Press, 1997.

_____. *Spiritual Warriors*. Sisters, OR: Multnomah Press, 2001.

_____. *Tender Warrior: God's Intention for a Man*. Sisters, OR: Multnomah Press, 1999.

Weidmann, Jim, Kurt Bruner, Mike Nappa and Amy Nappa. *An Introduction to Family Nights Tool Chest*. Colorado Springs. CO: Cook Communications, 1997.

Wheat, Ed and Gaye Wheat. *Intended for Pleasure: Sex Technique and Sexual Fulfillment in Christian Marriage*. Grand Rapids, MI: F. H. Revell, 1977.

Wiersbe, Warren W. *Be Strong: Putting God's Power to Work in Your Life*. Colorado Springs, CO: Chariot Victor Publishing, 1993.

Wilkerson, David. *Have You Felt Like Giving Up Lately*. Grand Rapids, MI: F. H. Revell, 1997.

Willard, Dallas. *The Spirit of the Disciplines*. San Francisco: HarperCollins, 1991.

Wright, H. Norman. *Making Peace With Your Past*. Grand Rapids, MI: Spire, 1997.

_____. *The Premarital Counseling Handbook*. 3rd ed. Chicago: Moody Press, 1992.

Wyrtzen, David. *Love Without Shame*. Grand Rapids, MI: Discovery House, 1991.

Yancey, Philip. *Prayer: Does it Make a Difference?* Grand Rapids, MI: Zondervan, 2006.

Ziglar, Zig. *Courtship After Marriage*. New York: Ballantine Books, 1990.

(ENDNOTES)

1   *TRADOC Mission* in *TRADOC*. Internet. Available at http://www-tradoc.army.mil/about.htm; accessed 12 February 2009.

2   Tim Kimmel, *Basic Training For a Few Good Men* (Nashville: Thomas Nelson, 1997), 29.

3   Gary Chapman, *The Four Seasons of Marriage* (Wheaton, IL: Tyndale House, 2005), 135.

4   Gary Smalley, *The DNA of Relationships* (Wheaton, IL: Tyndale House, 2004), 39.

5   Gary Smalley and John Trent, *The Blessing* (Nashville: Thomas Nelson, 1986), 67.

6   Linda and Charlie Bloom, *101 Things I Wish I Knew When I Got Married* (Novato, CA: New World Library, 2004), 19.

7   Gary Smalley, *Secrets to Lasting Love* (New York: Simon & Schuster, 2000), 96.

8   Christopher and Rachel McCluskey, *When Two Become One* (Grand Rapids: F. H. Revell, 2004), 36.

9   Smalley, *The DNA of Relationships*, 94.

10   Bloom, *101 Things I Wish I Knew When I Got Married*, 38.

11   Leonard Felder, *When Difficult Relatives Happen to Good People* (New York: Rodale, 2003), xiii.

12   Gary Smalley and John Trent, *The Language of Love* (Pomona, CA: Focus on the Family Publishing, 1988), 8.

13   Gary Smalley and John Trent, *The Hidden Value of a Man* (Wheaton, IL: Tyndale House, 1994), 117.

14   Gary Smalley and John Trent, *The Two Sides of Love* (Pomona, CA: Focus on the Family Publishing, 1990), 31.

15   Gary Chapman and Ross Campbell, *The Five Love Languages of Children* (Chicago: Northfield Publishing, 1997) 17.

16   Henry Cloud and John Townsend, *Boundaries in Marriage* (Grand Rapids, MI: Zondervan, 1999), 9.

17   All Scriptural quotations are from the *New International Version* (NIV) unless otherwise noted. *The New International Version Study Bible* (Grand Rapids: Zondervan, 1985).

18   Eric and Leslie Ludy, *The First 90 Days of Marriage* (Nashville: Thomas Nelson, 2006), xiii.

19   Larry Frolick, *Why Do People Divorce?* in *Divorce Magazine*. Internet. Available from http://www.divorcemag.com/ * ; accessed 15 January 2008.

20   Jim Killiam, *Don't Believe the Divorce Statistics* in *Christianity Today*. Internet. Available from http://www.christianitytoday.com/mp/7m2/7m2046.html; accessed 15 January 2008.

21   Ibid.

22   *Christians Divorce More Than Atheists* in *Religious Tolerance*. Internet. Available from http://www.religioustolerance.orf/chr_dira.h ; accessed 24 July 2007.

23   Ibid.

24   Ibid.

25   Ibid.

26   Ibid.

27   *Christians Divorce More Than Atheists* in *Religious Tolerance*. Internet. Available from http://www.religioustolerance.orf/chr_dira.h ; accessed 24 July 2007.

28   Ibid.

29   *The State of the Church* in *The Barna Update*. Internet. Available from http://www.barna.org/FlexPage.aspx?Page=BarnaUpdate&BarnaUpdateID=49; accessed 10 January 2008.

30   Samuele Bacchiocchi, *The Marriage Covenant* in *Biblical Perspectives*. Internet. Available from http://www.biblicalperspectives.com/books/marriage/2.html; accessed 15 January 2008.

31   Al Janssen, *The Covenant Marriage* in *Focus on the Family*, Internet. Available from http://www.family.org/marriage/A000001012.cfm; accessed 14 August 2007.

32   Ibid.

33   Gary Chapman, *Covenant Marriage* (Nashville: Broadman & Holman Publishing, 2003), 11.

34   Chapman, *Covenant Marriage*, 8.

35   Ibid.

36   Ibid.

37   John Bradshaw, *The Family* (Deerfield Beach, FL: Health Communications, 1996), 51.

38   Tim LaHaye, *Why You Act The Way You Do* (Wheaton, IL: Tyndale House, 1984), 21.

39   David Keirsey, *Please Understand Me II: Temperament, Character and Intelligence* (Del Mar, CA: Prometheus Nemesis, 1998), 21.

40   Ibid.

41   Marvin Minsky, *The Emotion Machine* (New York: Simon & Schuster, 2006), 17.

42   Florence Littauer, *Personality Plus* (Grand Rapids: F. H. Revell, 1992), 11.

43   Ibid., 57-60.

44   Tim LaHaye, *Transformed Temperament* (Wheaton, IL: Tyndale House, 1975), 9.

45   Littauer, *Personality Plus*, 86.

46   Myles Munroe, *The Purpose and Power of Love and Marriage* (Shippensburg, PA: Destiny Image Publishers, 2002), 155.

47   *Home Statistic* in *Statistics*. Internet. Available from http://www.cbs.nl/en-GB/menu/themas/mens-maatschappij/bevolking/publicaties/artikelen/2006-1862-wm.htm; accessed 29 August 2007.

48   Gary Smalley, *Change Your Heart, Change Your Life* (Nashville: Thomas Nelson, 2007), 209.

49   Ibid., 210.

50   *Evidences of Self Rejection* in *Family Support Link*. Internet. Available from http://ati.iblp.org/ati/supportlink/kb/questions/76/What+are+evidences+of+self-rejection%3F ; accessed 14 January 2008.

51   Matthew McKay and Patrick Fanning, *Self-Esteem,* 3rd ed. (Oakland, CA: Raincoast Books, 2000), 1-2.

52   Jim Denison, *The Self-Esteem Solution* in *God Issues*. Internet. Available from http://www.godissues.org/articles/articles/146/1/The-Self-esteem-Solution/Page1.html; accessed 15 January 2008.

53   *Evidences of Self Rejection* in *Family Support*. Internet. Available from http://ati.iblp.org/ati/supportlink/kb/questions/76/What+are+evidences+of+self-rejection%3F ; accessed 14 January 2008.

54   Bob Deffinbaugh, *The Qualities of a Godly Mate* in *Bible. Org*. Internet. Available from http://www.bible.org/page.php?page_id=642; accessed 8 October 2007.

55   *A Biblical Portrait of Marriage* in *Walk Thru the Bible*. Internet. Available from http://www.walkthru.org/site/News2?JServSessionIdr007=mo1skei39c.app7a&page=NewsArticle&id=5619; accessed 15 January 2008.

56   Richard Steel, *The Duties of a Husband and Wife* in *Eternal Life Ministries*. Internet. Available from (http://www.eternallifeministries. org/rs_duties.htm; accessed 8 October 2007.

57   Cloud, *Boundaries in Marriage*, 142.

58   Emerson Eggerichs, *Love and Respect* (Nashville: Integrity Publishers, 2004), 1.

59   Cloud, *Boundaries in Marriage,* 45.

60   Bob Lepine, *The Christian Husband: God's Vision for Loving and Caring for Your Wife* (Ann Arbor, MI: Servant Publications, 1999), 57.

61   Richard Steele, *The Duties of a Husband and Wife* in *Eternal Life Ministries.* Internet. Available from http://www.eternallifeministries.org/rs_duties.htm; accessed 8 October 2007.

62   Ibid.

63   Dennis Rainey, *Preparing for Marriage* (Little Rock: Gospel Light, 1997), 8.

64   David Brown, *Keep the Home Fires Burning* in *Logos Resource page.* Internet. Available from http://logosresourcepages.org/Family/pres-mar.htm; accessed 8 October 2007.

65   Carl Haak, *The Building of a Christian Home* in *The Reformed Witness Hour.* Internet. Available from http://www.prca.org/refwitness/1996/1996nov10.html; accessed 8 October 2007.

66   Del Tackett, *Why is a Christian Worldview Important* in *Focus on the Family.* Internet. Available from https://www.family.org/faith/A000001057.cfm; accessed 8 October 2007.

67   Parrott, *The Parent You Want to Be,* 153.

68   Ibid.

69   Ibid., 51.

70   Foster Cline and Jim Fay, *Parenting with Love and Logic* (Colorado Springs: Pino Press, 2006), 13.

71   *Christian Parenting—To Choose* in *Christian Parenting.* Internet. Available from http://www.allaboutparenting.org/christian-parenting.htm; accessed 8 October 2007.

72   Parrott, *The Parent You Want to Be,* 30.

73   Smalley, *Change Your Heart, Change Your Life,* 9.

74   Parrott, *The Parent You Want to Be,* 151.

75   McKay, *Self-Esteem,* 180.

76   *Biblical Parenting* in *Christian Parenting.* Internet. Available from http://www.allaboutparenting.org/biblical-parenting-faq.htm; accessed 8 October 2007.

77   Parrott, *The Parent You Want to Be,* 21.

78   Laura Schlessinger, *Bad Childhood, Good Life* (New York: HarperCollins, 2006), 3.

79   *Train Them Up* in *Focus on the Family.* Internet. Available from http://www.family.org/faith/A000000717.cfm; accessed 8 October 2007.

80   *Christian Parenting—To Choose* in *Christian Parenting. .* Internet. Available from http://www.allaboutparenting.org/christian-parenting.htm; accessed 8 October 2007.

81   Dave Ramsey, *Financial Peace Revisited* (New York: Viking, 2003), 195.

82   Ibid., 196.

83   Bill Bachrach, *Values-Based Financial Planning* (San Diego: Aim High Publishing, 2000), 4.

84   *His, Hers or Ours* in *Crown Financial Ministries*. Internet. Available from http://www.crown.org/library/ViewArticle.aspx?ArticleId=409; accessed 8 October 07.

85   *Marriage and Money* in *Focus on the Family*. Internet. Available from http://www.family.org/marriage/A000001828.cfm; accessed 8 October 07.

86   *The Merriam-Webster Dictionary,* 11 ed. (Springfield, MA: Merriam-Webster, Inc., 2005), 703.

87   *God and Money* in *Crown Financial Ministries*. Internet. Available from http://www.crown.org/library/ViewArticle.aspx?ArticleId=406; accessed 8 October 2007.

88   Larry Burkett, *How to Manage Your Money* (Chicago: Moody Press, 1975), 17.

89   *Overcoming Financial Issues* in *Popular Issues*. Internet. Available from http://www.allaboutpopularissues.org/financial-counseling-faq.htm; accessed 8 October 2007.

90   Larry Burkett, *Investing for the Future* (Wheaton, IL: Victory Books, 1996), 91.

91   Mitch Temple, *Adjusting to Marriage* in *Focus on the Family*. Internet. Available from http://www.family.org/marriage/A000001368.cfm; accessed 8 October 2007.

92   Tim LaHaye, *Spirit-Controlled Temperament* (Wheaton, IL: Tyndale House, 1984) 1.

93   Keirsey, *Please Understand Me II*, 20.

94   Littauer, *Personality Plus*, 11.

95   LaHaye, *Spirit-Controlled Temperament*, 2.

96   Keirsey, *Please Understand Me II*, 21.

97   Ibid., 3.

98   John C. Maxwell, *The 21 Irrefutable Laws of Leadership* (Nashville: Thomas Nelson, 1998), 64.

99   LaHaye, *Why You Act the Way You Do*, 23.

100   Littauer, *Personality Plus,* 146.

101   LaHaye, *Spirit-Controlled Temperament*, 7.

102   *The Divorce Statistics* in *CBS*. Internet. Available from http://www.cbs.nl/enGB/menu/themas/mens-aatschappij/bevolking/publicaties/artikelen/2006-1862-wm.htm; accessed 23 July 2006.

103   Keirsey, *Please Understand Me II*, 23.

104   Ibid., 25.

105   Smalley and Trent, *The Two Sides of Love*, 39.

106   Ibid., 49.

107   Ibid., 70

108   Littauer, *Personality Plus*, 31.

109   Smalley and Trent, *The Two Sides of Love,* 80.

110   Ibid., 84.

111   Ibid., 60.

112   Ibid., 64.

113   LaHaye, *Why You Act the Way You Do*, 37.

114   Ibid., 195.

115   Maxwell, *The 21 Indispensable Qualities of a Leader*, 89.

116   *The American Heritage Desk Dictionary and Thesaurus* (Boston: Houghton Mifflin Co., 2005), 143.

117   Gary and Norma Smalley, *Decide to Love* (Grand Rapids: Zondervan, 1985), 3.

118   Chapman, *The Five Love Languages,* 32.

119   Gottman, *Why Marriages Succeed or Fail*, 103-104.

120   Ibid., 73.

121   Willard F. Harley, Jr. *His Needs, Her Needs* (Grand Rapids: F. H. Revell, 2001), 66-67.

122   H. Norman Wright, *Communication: Key to Your Marriage* (Ventura, CA: Regal, 2000), 61.

123   Gary Chapman, *Now You Are Speaking My Language* (Nashville: Broadman & Holman Publishing Group, 2007), 7.

124   Gottman, *Why Marriages Succeed or Fail*, 28.

125   Ibid., 234.

126   Susan Forward, *Toxic In-Laws* (New York: HarperCollins, 2002), xi.

127   Forward, *Toxic In-Laws*, 176.

128   *Ten Basic Rules for Dealing With In-Laws* in *Family Education.* Internet. Available from http://life.familyeducation.com/in-laws/family/48061.html?detoured=1; accessed 19 January 2008.

129   Dina Koutas Poch, *I Love My In-Laws* (New York: Owl Books, 2007), 62.

130   Rainey, *Preparing for Marriage*, 96.

131   Lee Wilson, *The In's and Out's of Life With In-laws* in *Family Dynamics Institute.* Available from http://www.familydynamics.net/insandoutsoflifewithinlaws.htm; accessed 19 January 2008.

132   Ibid.

133   Henry Cloud and John Townsend, *How to Have That Difficult Conversation You've Been Avoiding* (Grand Rapids: Zondervan, 2005), 146.

134   Alyson Weasley, *The Role of Friendship in Marriage* in *Focus on the Family.* Internet. Available from http://www.family.org/marriage/A000003209.cfm; accessed 20 January 2008.

135   Ibid.

136   Bloom, *101 Things I Wish I Knew When I Got Married*, 113.

137   Maxwell, *The 21 Irrefutable Laws of Leadership*, 109.

138   Judy Starr, *The Enticement of the Forbidden* (Peachtree City, GA: Life ConnXions, 2004), 237.

139   Rainey, *Preparing for Marriage*, 187.

140   Chapman, *Covenant Marriage*, 148.

141   Bill Hybels and Rob Wilkins, *God's Gift of Sexual Intimacy: Tender Love* (Chicago: Moody Press, 1993), 14.

142   Ibid., 15.

143   McCluskey, *When Two Become One*, 78.

144   Ibid., 80.

145   Ibid., 81.

146   Dallas Willard, *The Spirit of the Disciplines* (San Francisco: HarperCollins, 1991), 77.

147   Clift and Kathleen Richards, *Knowing God Intimately* (Tulsa, OK: Victory House, 2001), 209.

148   *Parents Accepting Responsibility for Child's Spiritual Development* in *The Barna Group*. Internet. Available from http://www.barna.org/FlexPage.aspx?Page=BarnaUpdate&BarnaUpdateID=138; accessed 21 January 2008.

149   Adults Who Attend Church as a Child in The Barna Group. Internet. Available from http://www.barna.org/FlexPage.aspx?Page=BarnaUpdate&BarnaUpdateID=101; accessed 22 January 2008.

150   *Prayer* in *The Barna Group*. Internet. Available from http://www.barna.org/FlexPage.aspx?Page=BarnaUpdate&BarnaUpdateID=268; accessed 22 January 2008.

151   Philip Yancey, *Prayer: Does it Make a Difference?* (Grand Rapids: Zondervan, 2006), 118.

152   Ibid., 159.

153   Bill Hybels, *Too Busy Not to Pray* (Leicester, UK: InterVarsity Press, 1994), 12.

154   Terry Wardle, *Wounded* (Camp Hill, PA: Christian Publication, 1994), 43.

155   Ken Sande, *The Peace Maker*, rev. ed. (Grand Rapids: Baker Books, 2004), 204.

156   Ibid., 206-207.

157   Phillip McGraw, *Self Matters* (New York: Free Press, 2001), 110

158   Ibid.

159   Robert S. McGee, *The Search for Significance* (Nashville: Word Publishing, 1998), 3.

160   David and Karen Mains, *Building Your Mate's Self Esteem*

(Ventura, CA.: Gospel Light, 1997), 33.

161   Munroe, *The Purpose and Power of Love and Marriage*, 132.

162   McGee, *The Search For Significance*, 20.

163   Deborah Newman, *Developing a Healthy Body Image* in *Focus on the Family*. Internet. Available from http://www.oneplace.com/Ministries/Focus_on_the_Family/Archives.asp?bcd=2007-4-25; accessed 17 May 2007.

164   Munroe, *The Purpose and Power of Love and Marriage*, 144.

165   John L. Mason, *You're Born an Original, Don't Die a Copy* (Altamonte Springs, FL: Insight International, 1993), 13.

166   McKay, *Self-Esteem*, 89.

167   Dixie Ruth Crase, Arthur H. Criscoe, *Parenting By Grace: Discipline and Spiritual Growth* (Nashville: Lifeway Press, 1995), 22.

168   Ibid., 179.

169   H. Norman Wright, *Making Peace With Your Past* (Grand Rapids: Spire, 1997), 76.

170   Ibid., 77.

171   James Dobson, *What Wives Wish Their Husbands Knew About Women* (Wheaton, IL: Living Books, 1975), 28.

172   Smalley, *The Blessing*, 9.

173   Rainey, *Building Your Mate's Self-Esteem* , 54.

174   Ibid., 55.

175   Dobson, *What Wives Wish Their Husbands Knew About Women*, 24-25.

176   Gene A. Getz, *The Measure of a Woman* (Ventura, CA: Regal, 1977), 13-14.

177   Dobson, *What Wives Wish Their Husbands Knew About Women*, 26-27.

178   Ibid., 28-34.

179   Donald M. Joy, *Bonding: Relationships in the Image of God* (Nappanee, IN: Evangel, 1999), 63.

180   Kaja Perina, *Relationships: Low Self-Esteem Hurts* in *Psychology Today Magazine*. Internet. Available from http://psychologytoday.com/articles/pto-20030711-000002.html; accessed 17 May 2007.

181   Rainey, *Building Your Mate's Self Esteem*, 55-60.

182   David and Karen Mains, *Living, Loving, Leading* (Weston, Ontario, Canada: Cook Publishing, 1992), 29.

183   Dietrich Bonhoeffer, *Life Together* (San Francisco: HarperCollins, 1954), 22.

184   Donald S. Whitney, *Spiritual Disciplines for the Christian Life* (Colorado Springs: NavPress, 1991), 17.

185   Bill Phillips, *Body for Life* (New York: HarperCollins, 1999), 33.

186   R. Kent Hughes, *Disciplines of a Godly Man* (Wheaton, IL: Crossway Books, 2001), 14.

187   William Carr Peel, *The Character of a Christian: Design for Discipleship* (Colorado Springs: NavPress, 1980), 5.

188   Rick Warren, *The Purpose Driven Life* (Grand Rapids, MI: Zondervan, 2002), 17.

189   James Dobson, *Prescription of a Successful Marriage* in *Focus on the Family*. Internet. Available from http://www.family.org/marriage/A000000987.cfm; accessed 10 May 2007.

190   Max Lucado, *Turn* (Sisters, OR: Multnomah, 2005), 53.

191   James Dobson, *Love for a Lifetime* (Sisters, OR: Multnomah, 1998), 51.

192   Hybels, *Too Busy Not To Pray*, 60.

193   Ibid., 62.

194   T.W. Hunt, *The Doctrine of Prayer* (Nashville: Convention Press, 1986), 8.

195   William Carr Peel, *What God Does When Men Pray* (Colorado Springs: NavPress, 1993), 61.

196   Lucado, *Turn*, 42.

197   Richards, *Knowing God Intimately*, 177.

198   Dietrich Bonhoeffer, *The Cost of Discipleship* (New York: Simon & Schuster, 1995), 63.

199   John R.W. Stott, *Basic Christianity,* 2nd ed. (Grand Rapids: William B. Eerdmans, 1971), 112.

200   C.S. Lewis, *A Grief Observed* (San Francisco: HarperCollins, 1996), 60.

201   Henry T. Blackaby and Claude V. King, *Experiencing God* (Nashville: Broadman & Holman, 1994), 113.

202   Bill Gothard, *Basic Life Principles* in *Institutes for Basic Life Principles*. Internet. Available from http://search.atomz.com/search/?sp-q=life+conflicts&sp-a=sp10023b3a&sp-f=ISO-8859-1&search.x=11&search.y=11; accessed 15 May 2007.

203   Ibid.

204   Charles Swindoll, *Quotes* in *Brainy Quotes*. Internet. Available from http://www.brainyquote.com/quotes/authors/c/charles_r_swindoll.html; accessed 20 May 2007

205   Oswald Chambers, *My Utmost for His Highest* (Grand Rapids: Discovery House, 1992), 45.

206   Charles Swindoll, *Spiritual Gifts* (Waco, TX: Word Publishing, 1986), 39.

207 Rick Warren, *Purpose Driven Marriage* in *Christianity Today*. Internet. Available from http://www.christianitytoday.com/mp/2004/002/1.26.html; accessed 20 May 2007.

208 Mains, *Living, Loving, Leading*, 9.

209 Ibid.,10.

210 James Dobson, *Prescription for a Successful Marriage* in *Focus on The Family*. Internet. Available from http://www.family.org/marriage/A000000987.cfm; accessed 10 May 2007.

211 Mains, *Living, Loving, Leading*, 19.

212 Hughes, *Disciplines of a Godly Man*, 35.

213 Carol Heffernan, *Relational Needs* in *Focus on The Family*. Internet. Available from http://www.family.org/marriage/A000001386.cfm; accessed 18 May 2007.

214 Hughes, *Disciplines of a Godly Man*, 38.

215 Carol Heffernan, *Relational Needs* in *Focus on The Family*. Internet. Available from http://www.family.org/marriage/A000001386.cfm; accessed 18 May 2007.

216 Carol Heffernan, *Bringing New Life to Your Marriage* in *Focus on The Family*. Internet. Available from http://www.family.org/marriage/A000001385.cfm; accessed 14 May 2007.

217 Kimmel, *Basic Training for a Few Good Men*, 141.

218 *The House's Foundation* in *House Tips*. Internet. Available from http://hometips.com/hyhw/structure/106found.html; accessed 1 June 2007.

219 Carol Heffernan, *God's Design for Marriage* in *Focus on The Family*. Internet. Available from http://www.family.org/marriage/A000001011.cfm; accessed 2 June 2007.

220 Munroe, *The Purpose and Power of Love and Marriage*, 19.

221 Dobson, *Love for a Lifetime*, 10.

222 Ibid., 11.

223 John Gray, *Men are From Mars and Women are From Venus* (New York: HarperCollins, 1992), 59-60.

224 Munroe, *The Purpose and Power of Love and Marriage*, 19.

225 James Dobson, *Seven Keys to Lifelong Love* in *Focus on the Family*. Internet. Available from http://www.family.org/marriage/A000000988.cfm ; accessed 29 May 2007.

226 Jerry Jenkins, *Loving Your Marriage Enough To Protect It* (Chicago: Moody Press, 1993), 14.

227 Dobson, *Love for a Lifetime*, 10.

228 David and Claudia Arp, *Partners or Parents* in *Christianity Today*. Internet. Available from http://www.christianitytoday.com/mp/7m3/7m3016.html; accessed 28 May 2007.

229 James Dobson, *The New Hide and Seek* (Grand Rapids: F. H. Revell, 2007), 224.

230   *America's Children in Brief: Key National Indicators of Well-Being—2006* in *Childstats*. Internet. Available from http://childstats.gov/pubs. asp; accessed 30 May 2007.

231   Sal Severe, *How to Behave So Your Children Will Too* (New York: Penguin Books, 2003), 21.

232   Ibid., 22-23.

233   Dorothy Law Nolte and Rachel Harris, *Children Learn What They Live* (New York: Workman,1998), ix.

234   Ibid., xvi.

235   Tommy Nelson, *The Essentials of a Healthy Home* in *Focus on Your Child*. Internet. Available from http://www.focusonyourchild.com/faith/art1/A0000522.html; accessed 29 May 2007.

236   Helen Neville and Diane Clark Johnson, *Temperament Tools: Working With Your Child's Inborn Traits* (Seattle, WA: Parenting Press, 1998), 11-13.

237   Chapman, *5 Love Languages of Children*, 8.

238   Ibid., 27.

239   James Dobson, *Parenting the Strong-Willed Child* (New York: Contemporary Books, 2002), 167.240   Bruce Van Patter, *Parents and Children* in *Focus on the Family*; Internet. Available from http://www.family.org/parenting/A0000004l2.cfm; accessed 19 May 2007.

241   Gary Smalley, *Homes of Honor* (Branson, MO: Smalley Relationship Center, 1996), 73.

242   Dobson, *The New Hide and Seek*, 122.

243   David R. Miller, *Tough Kids* (Elgin, IL: Christian Parenting Books, 1993), 146.244   Jim Mhoon, *A Parent's Challenge* in *Focus on The Family*. Internet. Available from http://www.family.org/parenting/A000000678.cfm; accessed 19 May 2007.

245   Bob Barnes, *Minute Meditations for Men* (Eugene, OR: Harvest House, 1998), 231.

246   T. Berry Brazelton, *Touchpoints* (New York: Addison-Wesley, 1992), 253.

247   Dobson, *The New Hide and Seek*, 123.

248   Karen Miller, *Tailor-Made Discipline* in *Christian Parenting Today*. Internet. Available from http://store.christianparentingtodaystore.com/freesamples.html; accessed 30 May 2007.

249   Ibid.

250   *Bless Your Children* in *Focus on Your Child*. Internet. Available from http://www.focusonyourchild.com/relation/art1/A0000359.html; accessed 30 May 2007.

251   Gary Smalley, *The Blessing*, 41.

252   Ibid., 50.

253   Ibid., 69.

254   Ibid., 82.

255   Smalley, *The Blessing*, 100-101.

256   Barnes, *Meditations for Men*, 18.

257   Jesse Florea, *Say Your Prayers* in *Focus on Your Children*. Internet. Available from http://www.focusonyourchild.com/faith/art1/A0000524.html; accessed 30 May 2007.

258   Dutch Sheets, *Intercessory Prayer* (Ventura, CA: Regal Books, 1997), 207.

259   Karen Scalf Linamen, *The Parent Warrior: Doing Spiritual Battle for Your Children* (Wheaton, IL: Victory Books, 1993), 33.

260   Ester Ilnisky, *Let the Children Pray* in *Christian Parenting Today*. Internet. Available from http://www.christianitytoday.com/cpt/2001/004/7.42.html; accessed 30 May 2007.

261   Bachrach, *Values-Based Financial Planning*, xvi.

262   Burkett, *How to Manage Your Money*, 4.

263   Ibid., 17.

264   *Controlling Impulsive and Compulsive Spending* in *Focus on The Family*. Internet. Available from http://www.family.org/lifechallenges/A000002038.cfm; accessed 2 June 2007.

265   *Financial Authority* in *Focus on The Family*. Internet. Available from http://www.family.org/marriage/A000001831.cfm; accessed 29 May 2007.

266   *Learning Contentment* in *Focus on The Family*. Internet. Available from http://www.family.org/lifechallenges/A000002037.cfm; accessed 30 may 2007.

267   Ibid.

268   Burkett, *How to Manage Your Money*, 13.

269   Ron Blue, *Mastering Your Money in Marriage* (Little Rock, AR: Family Ministry, 1990), 42.

270   *History: The Bristol Miracle* in *George Muller Foundation*. Internet. Available from http://www.mullers.org/history.html#A%20TEST%20OF%20FAITH; accessed 30 May 2007.

271   Burkett, *How to Manage Your Money*, 65.

272   *Tithing When Your Spouse Objects* in *Focus on The Family*. Internet. Available from http://www.family.org/marriage/A000001832.cfm; accessed 30 May 2007.

273   Burkett, *How to Manage Your Money*, 111.

274   Blue, *Mastering Your Money in Marriage*, 53.

275   Ibid., 26.

276   Barnes, *Meditations for Men*, 149.

277   *Tithing When Your Spouse Objects* in *Focus on The Family*. Internet. Available from http://www.family.org/marriage/A000001832.cfm; accessed 30 May 2007.

278   Burkett, *How to Manage Your Money*, 127.

279   *God's Minimum Financial Standards for Couples* in *Focus on The Family*. Internet. Available from http://www.family.org/marriage/A000001829.cfm; accessed 30 May 2007.

280   *Born-Again Christians Just As Likely to Divorce As Are Non-Christians* in *The Barna Group*. Internet. Available from *http://www.barna.org/FlexPage.aspx?Page=BarnaUpdate&BarnaUpdateID=170;* accessed 23 July 2006.

281   Sharon Jayson, *Premarital Education Could Cut Divorce Rate, Survey Finds* in *USA Today*. Internet. Available from http://www.usatoday.com/news/education/2006-06-21-premarital-education_x.htm; accessed 24 July 2007.

282   Donna Miles, *Army Divorce Rates Drop as Marriage Programs Gain Momentum* in *American Forces Press Service*. Internet. Available from http://www.defenselink.mil/news/Jan2006/20060127_4034.html; accessed 24 July 2007.

283   Louis A. Ferrebee, *The Healthy Marriage Handbook* (Nashville: Holman, 2001), 195.

284   Ibid., 203.

285   Gary Chapman, *Home Improvements* (Carol Steam, IL: Tyndale House, 2006), 91.

PUBLISHED *by* PARABLE!
Earthly Stories with a Heavenly Meaning